Dedicated to my Dream Makers Group
~Making Dreams Come True~

Caughlin Consulting
Houston, Texas 77025

Edited by Lisa Birman

Cover designs & Photography by William T. Cannady

Design by David Richmond

The Art of Waking Up

40 Days to Awaken Your Brain

Your Step by Step Guide to Transform Negative Thoughts and Feelings

By

Angela Caughlin, LCSW

The Art of Waking Up

40 Days to Awaken Your Brain

Your Step by Step Guide to Transform Negative Thoughts and Feelings

Prologue

Introduction

Prologue

My name is Angela. I was a wife and a mother of three young children when my husband, whom I cared for more than anything else in the world, died. His death was tragic and devastating, thrusting me out of what had been my ordinary existence. As I grew to understand and embrace my journey through grief's spiraling maze, I learned extraordinary lessons.

In my desperation to keep my head on straight during Tom's illness, and then reeling from his death, I started journaling. Anne Frank wrote in her diary, "I can shake off anything as long as I can write; my sorrows disappear, my courage is reborn." I felt the same way. This was long before we **really** knew what journaling could do! I did not understand why, I just knew I had to write. I had no idea that journaling would be become my "best friend" and contribute to saving my health and my life. I wrote about the good, the bad, and the ugly. I wrote letters to God. When I was quiet enough to listen, I got answers.

I realized that I felt better after I wrote. I was able to face the day without crying. I could actually be present. Eventually, I started writing about my desires. I wrote about the things I was grateful for; I wrote about my dreams. I listened for answers. I now know this is the key to moving forward.

Words trigger emotions and activate particular chemicals. It's important to download and get in touch with those deep, yucky feelings. But staying focused on those negative thoughts keeps us stuck in the past. It's a delicate balance. We have to dig deep and feel those gut-wrenching emotions to get through them. Emotion is like a wave. It will come crashing in on the shore and always go rolling back out. But sometimes, like a surfer, we have to fall off of our board, get up, and ride the wave back out. Like the wave, your emotions don't have to get stuck. Journaling lets you move through the emotions, then ride the wave to what comes next.

Journaling helped me get in touch with my "real life." It made it impossible to minimize or ignore my habits and patterns—they were staring back at me from the page. I found myself rehashing the same material day by day, and would think, "Didn't I just write that yesterday?" Like my own reality show, I was writing my story one day at a time. Unfortunately, sometimes my story would sometimes get stuck. I would get bogged down in the past.

This awareness of my patterns was the jolt I needed to make a conscious choice to change. That is the biggest gift journaling brought me—the ability to see new choices, to hear my own voice, allowing me to change and transform. I believe it can bring the same gift to your life.

Journaling takes courage, but it also gives us courage! As the potential to change looms large, our dreams start to take form. We see our self walking out of our past, putting one foot in front of the other and going through a new door, honoring what we have learned. Your journal is a safe and fertile container for your dreams. It won't negate them like your thinking mind might. It won't try to talk you out of something, like a well-meaning friend who is afraid that you might fail or be disappointed. Journaling is soul work.

As you explore your dreams, you'll start to connect the dots and move through the unknown with synchronicity and possibility.

In my work as a therapist, I have found that there is a lot of confusion about how to make changes. I often hear, "What is the easiest way through this? I just want it to be over." Another common response is, "I have tried this or that technique and it doesn't work." I understand why people give up on change. It's hard work. There are so many options and so much information. As I dug deeper, I began to understand that there is no magic pill. The answer is not "just journaling" or "just mindfulness." The broader understanding of the cosmos has led to a greater understanding of the connections between science and spirituality. Together these work in tandem to support us in our movements and contribute to making the long -term sustainable changes we are hoping to make a part of our everyday lives.

In this journal, I have collected information from various realms in a format that is easy to digest and navigate. As you work through the material, you'll investigate your own patterns and find yourself able to make incremental positive changes in your life.

Making positive long-lasting change is no small task. Changing your health may involve changing your relationships, your career, or finances. It can be daunting to consider all the micro and macro systems at play. But, at the same time, you'll realize how very important every thought and decision are, and how they impact everything around you. It's all designed to work together.

I invite you to take this journey of transformation with me. Together, we'll unwind old negative tapes and tap into the Universe's natural flow of changing from one season to the next. Let's get started on the road to waking up. Let's move away from negative thoughts and beliefs and toward affirmation and happiness. Over the next forty days, I invite you to welcome change into your life and step into the possibilities of your full potential!

Introduction

The Art of Waking Up

Many of us feel, at one time or another, that we are sleepwalking through our lives. We notice the repetitious negative thought patterns we live in, but feel powerless to change them. The ability to change negative thoughts and feelings is determined by only one thing—how fully we are awake and living in the present.

This book is a guide to truly waking up. It is a step-by-step journey designed to help you uncover the truth of your own negative thoughts, feelings, beliefs, motivations, patterns, actions, reactions, perceptions, and interpretations. It will show you how to use precise information and tools from the worlds of science and spirituality to begin to create the changes that are most important to you in living an awakened life.

In my career as a psychotherapist over the past twenty years, I have met hundreds of clients. In all that time, I have never met one who didn't have a desire to change, to clean out the "junk." But desire is not enough. If we continue to think and react within old and familiar negative patterns, we'll continue to experience the same reality. The true challenge is being willing to identify, understand, and actually change the negative thoughts and feelings that drive harmful behavior patterns. It takes courage to discover new ways of thinking and feeling.

In our everyday lives, our values and beliefs, our internal forces, are shaped by the way we think, feel, and perceive.

These core beliefs are often fueled by negative thoughts and feelings that are unexamined and unconscious. In this journal we will identify those feelings, as well as the universal patterns—both scientific and spiritual—that can wake us up to our true power and purpose. We will also explore the intersections of current spiritual teaching and contemporary science, illuminating the grand design of our lives and the many profound ways in which we are connected to one another.

Understanding the truth of our own story and beliefs enables us to change. Over the years, it has become clear to me that people who have an awareness of the interconnection of body, mind, and spirit are able to see themselves as part of a greater whole. This understanding greatly expands their capacity to embrace a new vision of themselves. They are able to see what is possible—not only in their personal lives, but in the larger world. To remove blocks and create positive patterns of change, we must open the door to a new perception of our own experiences in the present moment.

Science, consciousness, and spirituality are becoming surprisingly comfortable bedfellows. The call to each of us to become active agents in changing our own individual lives and the life of the planet is getting louder. Awakening requires that we look at all aspects of this paradigm shift to understand its relevance to our lives, our thoughts and beliefs, and to our ability to make profound and lasting changes. Richard Rohr says, "Now that we are coming to understand the magnificent nature of the cosmos, we're finding that many of the intuitions of the mystics of all religions are being paralleled by scientific theories and explanations. If truth is one (which it has to somehow be, if it is truth), then all disciplines are just approaching that truth from different angles and levels and questions."

This journal highlights our ability to make sustainable life changes by changing the neural pathways in our brains. The scientific exploration of this interconnectedness is ongoing, as are numerous studies on the effect of negative thoughts and emotions on our DNA. Scientific studies are also measuring the changes in brain activity during meditation and journaling. The bodies that make us tick and the modalities that help us to change are interdependent. They are all working together.

The 40-Day Work Plan
Given that we have a limited amount of time and energy each day, breaking out of old rote negative thought patterns can seem almost impossible. So we need to make it simple. In this journal I offer a step-by-step guide for daily journaling and a template to create a **40-Day Daily Conscious Living Plan** to help you achieve the changes you want to make.

The first step is to get a journal or notebook or create a private document on your computer or tablet to record your responses. This is a correspondence with yourself. Remember, it does not have to be perfect. Pick a physical location in which to write that works for you. It might be a certain room in your house, a coffee shop, or somewhere in nature. Just find a spot that allows you a little space to think.

The second step is to read over the seven categories of the Daily Conscious Living Plan:
      1. Relationships

2. Money/Finance
3. Spirituality
4. Work/Career/Vocation
5. Play
6. Health
7. Creativity

You are going to decide which categories resonate the most with you. It is difficult to work on more than **one or two** areas at a time, so be selective about which categories seem the most important to you right now.

The third step is to write a vision for each of the categories that you picked. You will be given instructions about how to do this on Day 3. You will then have a compass for where you are headed.

The fourth step, on Day 4, is to pick one or two things to work on in each category you select. Think about small movements you can make to change your focus and support your vision. You will be engaging in these movements every day. Over time, the movement should begin to feel like a new rhythm.

Throughout the 40 days you will find journaling exercises called **Try It Now Writing Exercises**. These exercises will help you gain clarity about what you want and why. They are designed to lead you down necessary paths to uncover your negative thoughts and patterns and discover your true feelings and emotions. They will ignite your body, mind, and spirit to reconnect and awaken you. New brain science tells us that conscious mind programming will support you in moving through your own resistance, bringing not just temporary change, but lasting change.

These exercises will help you refine your unique **Daily Conscious Living Plan.** Your **Daily Conscious Living Plan** is a customized plan that uses tools from both contemporary science and ancient spiritual wisdom to help you make lasting, measurable changes in your life in only **40 days.** This is more than just goal setting. This is making conscious choices to unearth and change negative patterns, adding new positive thoughts and experiences, and being aware of the feelings you evoke in yourself by changing these patterns.

By creating this plan and committing to these practices for **40 days**, you will become more Awake. You will operate in the present, where change can happen. Your negative thought patterns, your feelings, your brain, your awareness, and your life will begin to change and you will recognize parts of yourself that have been dormant for far too long. This plan will help you reclaim and rebuild a rich inner life, with thoughts and feelings that help you step into a flow that connects you to smart choices, clarity, happiness, and purpose.

At the end of the journal, you'll find a **Worksheet** to track your **Daily Conscious Living Plan,** for those of you who want to keep track of your changes on a point system. Some of us need this and others do not. It is totally up to you.

Why 40 Days?
Numbers have spiritual significance. Forty is an especially powerful number. It is not just the number of hours in a work week or the number of spaces on a Monopoly game board; in many ancient spiritual and religious traditions the number forty is the number of waiting, the number of

preparation. In the Bible the number forty is mentioned one hundred times and is used to start a new chapter of history. The Kabbalah tells us that it takes forty days to ingrain new ways of being into our systems. In science, negative forty (or forty-below) is the unique temperature at which the Celsius and Fahrenheit scales of measuring temperature connect. The average term of a pregnancy is forty weeks. In numerology, forty holds the vibration of higher consciousness. It is the only number whose letters are in alphabetical order. In many yogic and human consciousness practices it is widely accepted that it takes forty days to break or change a habit. For these reasons and many more, the number forty is a strategic number in creating personal transformation.

The Role of Science
Understanding more about how the scientific universe works—Neuroplasticity, the role of DNA, Epigenetics, Heartmath and the impact negative thoughts and emotions have in our lives—can help us on our journey towards wakefulness. Contemporary science is exploding with new information about how the physical universe works, and many of these discoveries can be distilled into practical information and tools to help us see ourselves in a new and powerful light.

Over the next forty days, we'll explore some incredible scientific breakthroughs. We'll look at neuroscience and the amazing capacity of the brain to transform, evolve, and heal itself. We'll examine the fascinating new field of Epigenetics, involving stimuli of DNA by signals outside the cells, including positive and negative thoughts. We'll talk about Hearthmath and the impact of emotion on health, intelligence, and awareness. We'll learn about fractal geometry and its role in redefining the structure of everything from your cells to the stars. Exploring these scientific connections will help us see the potential in the physical universe and harness that potential to create lasting change in our own minds, bodies, and spirits.

This level of transformation is not simply about changing your mind or deciding to live differently, it is about creating a conscious smart plan to rewire the new neural pathways attached to feelings and experiences that, quite literally, and naturally, change your brain.

The Role of Spirit
Identifying our true spiritual values is an important part of our transformational work. There are many views of God, and many different ways of defining and understanding our deep connection to the Divine and the meaning that has in each of our individual lives. As we determine the changes we want to make, the role of Spirit/God, has a direct impact on our values and "why" we want to make certain changes.

I have always been drawn to Carl Jung's work because of the expansive insight he offers into the worlds of medicine/science and spirituality. His work with the conscious, unconscious, collective unconscious, and dreams and archetypes has been the basis of groundbreaking work for numerous scientific and spiritual scholars. We will examine the work of other important thinkers, including Joseph Campbell's theories of the Monomyth and Hero's Journey. Identifying the core messages of spiritual masters and teachers, such as Gandhi, Jesus, Buddha, and Mother Teresa, can help us define the beliefs we live from.

The long road to living an awake, conscious life is filled with setbacks and obstacles that many want to resist. Changing negative thoughts and feelings and letting go of old tapes from the past is how we break ground to live in the present. We may be tempted to turn back to the familiar rather than going to the edge and moving through a situation. What we know always seems far safer and easier than what we don't know. Somehow, as we Awaken, turning back is no longer an option.

Finding Your Story

In this journal, you will begin your day-to-day journey toward changing negative thoughts and feelings by looking at your own story. Your story is first marked by the DNA that resides within you in a configuration that is as singular as your own fingerprints. DNA is the common denominator we share with all living things, with which we are intrinsically and forever connected. But, contrary to popular belief, our genes are not necessarily our destiny.

Your family of origin is an important part of your DNA and your story. The choices that are made for you, and the ones that you continue to make, activate the potentiality of your DNA in ways that shape your physical health, negative thoughts and feelings, mental capabilities, and who you believe yourself to be. Understanding the context of your story will help orient you to a greater understanding of the choices that were made for you, how you responded to those choices and, ultimately, what drives how you make choices today.

Clues in both the scientific and spiritual realms allow us to understand that we are a part of something greater. In order to expand beyond our limited selves, transform negative thoughts and feelings, and make changes toward a new vision, we must understand how to align with nature and access the power of the infinite, eternal creative forces of the Universe. We must awaken the magic within us to connect with the magic that surrounds us.

Our lives can be chaotic tangles of wants, fears, hopes, hates, and loves—a lifelong chain of actions and reactions created by our negative thoughts or feelings, many painful, that shape the way we live, work, love, and play. When we become aware of these actions or reactions we often focus on the ones that cause us anxiety and harm. We know that improving the quality of our lives depends on changing these behaviors. And yet we seldom take the time to discover their causes. Uncovering their origins, finding out what truly causes us to act and react as we do, is the key that unlocks the change we are longing for. It is this key that allows us to live the life we desire.

Many stories—both in myth and in real life—tell of a significant event that prompts us to begin the Journey into the Unknown. Often this story is reflective of a painful event. Other stories begin when we realize we can no longer live the life we are living. It is scary to uncover what we have worked so diligently to hide—not just from others, but also from ourselves. We are all called to the Unknown at some point in our lives. Some of us go willingly, and some of us are forced into the Journey. After we have entered the Unknown, we are presented with many challenges and situations that make us dig deep—soul deep. This depth is where waking up and examining the negative thought patterns that drive us truly begins.

Transforming the Whole

Whatever we are trying to change—our eating habits, our lifestyle, career, relationships, meditative practice, or our happiness level—we cannot change just one thing without changing and being attentive to the effect it will have on all parts of our life. To begin, we need to look at the areas that are ripe for change, and make a commitment to practice these shifts in our daily living for a period of **40 Days.** If you have picked up this guided journal, you are ready to change your negative thoughts and feelings, discover your own truth, live in the present, and Wake Up!

Day 1

My Unique Self: Metamorphosis and Your Family of Origin

The privilege of a lifetime is being who you are.
– Joseph Campbell

Every living species on this planet is wired for change. Waking up to conscious change means simply realizing that your life is not where you want it to be and making a plan for how to get it there. The greatest gift that we receive from creating change in our lives is the ability to live fully in the present moment. But simply saying that you are ready to change is not enough. Our negative thoughts and feelings are deeply rooted in our psyche, so we must be brave enough to uproot our own core patterns in order to live our lives differently. We must be brave enough to Awaken.

Metamorphosis

So what makes us do the things we do? Is it our DNA, our life experiences, our thoughts, our beliefs, or a little of everything? The Monarch butterfly travels each year from the exact same locations throughout the US and Canada, finally reaching its destination thousands of miles later in the remote Sierra Madre Mountains of Michoacan, Mexico. These beautiful creatures know exactly where to go and what to do because of their DNA. It is imprinted in the wings of every butterfly.

Every chromosome in our body is filled with tightly coiled strands of DNA, it is the common denominator of every living organism. The families we are born into determine our DNA. As individuals, we each have a unique genetic blueprint. But, contrary to popular belief, recent research shows that our genes do not wholly dictate our destiny. Studies now show that the lifestyle choices we make profoundly influence the expression of our genes. Certain experiments, described below, can show us the paradigm shift that is now occurring in our understanding of DNA. This is the new frontier of human metamorphosis. We are transforming—as individuals, as a human species, and as a planet.

If we desire to truly change our lives, if we want to shift our negative thoughts and feelings out of auto-pilot and into making conscious choices to Awaken, we must be willing to examine and let go of many of the thoughts, feelings, and beliefs that arise from our families of origin. That can be a bit scary, like letting go of an old friend. Living fully in the present moment requires that we let go of old negative thoughts and feelings that are simply no longer true. Our long-held beliefs may no longer be congruent with who we are today. So how do we let go of these negative thoughts and feelings that no longer serve us?

Your Family of Origin
It is surprising the number of people who don't know the details about the most important moment of their life— their birth. How did you enter the world? Wanted or not, the belief systems that were handed to you from your family seep into your reality. You can't change what you don't understand, so digging into the details of your birth environment is the first step.

Contemporary science claims that—even in utero—we are aware of the feelings and environment within our family of origin. Acknowledging the things that have been handed to us, but no longer work for us, is the first step in making conscious choices to change and begin the process of Awakening.

Some negative thoughts and feelings are created from the "scripts" and beliefs held and perpetuated within a family. An example of a family "script" or belief might be: "There will never be enough money to afford the things we need." Many old scripts no longer apply. What are the scripts you inherited from your family? What are the things your family does that you do not want to do anymore?

As you start to examine your stories, you'll become aware of the choices that you've made—and the choices that were made for you. These choices could be cultural beliefs or assumptions about your family that are largely unconscious. Or they could be habits and beliefs that appear to morph and recur in your own life. Family scripts play a big part in blocking our ability to receive what we say we want in life. Sometimes we have to look at the repetitious patterns in multiple generations of our family before we can understand how we are repeating the same traits. Take some time to think about what family scripts might be playing out in your life and holding you back from achieving your dream.

Focusing on your birth family as we begin this work will help you to discover how your birth story links with the present moment in which you find yourself today. This is the first puzzle piece in uncovering the big picture of who you really are.

Try It Now Writing Exercise #1
Where and when were you born?

_____

_____

_____

_____

_____

_____

_____

Who was there?

_____

_____

_____

_____

_____

_____

_____

Was the birth difficult or easy?

_____

_____

_____

_____

_____

_____

Add any details that you know about the story of your birth.

_____

_____

_____

_____

_____

Try It Now Writing Exercise #2
Is there a script or belief that you feel you have inherited from your family?

_____
_____
_____
_____
_____
_____
_____

What would happen if you let go of certain family scripts?

_____
_____
_____
_____
_____
_____
_____

What negative thoughts could you let go of in letting go of those scripts?

_____
_____
_____
_____
_____
_____
_____

The next time that script comes into your mind, say out loud, "That is not true," and see what happens. Consider what truth might replace that outdated or untrue family script. Write it here now so that you can bring it to mind later.

_____

_____

_____

_____

_____

_____

_____

My Daily Practice
- **Try It Now Writing Exercises #1, #2.**

Journal:
- **Journal 15 to 30 minutes.**
- **Set an intention for the day that reflects a change you'd like to bring into your life.**
- **Visualize yourself doing this activity. Really feel it!**
- **Happy List: Write about one thing that went well today. What made you happy or grateful? Anything counts— even a good cup of coffee! Close your eyes and feel this feeling throughout your body! Start a "Happy List" and make this your first entry!**

Day 2

My Roots: Family of Origin

A people without the knowledge of their past history, origin, and culture is like a tree without roots.
– Marcus Garvey

As you dig a little deeper, you can heighten your awareness of family dynamics. Try thinking about it as though you are an outsider peering in through a window. You get to choose what values, scripts, attitudes, love, and communications you want to adopt going forward. It is a choice!

Shifting your current mindset means being open to overriding the way your mind has been conditioned by past experiences. It is important to believe that you can have a different life experience. If you continue to work out of an old family system that relies on the predictors of your parents or grandparents, you will never break free.

Your goal is transformation. That means rewiring your neurological circuitry of who you are, and perhaps altering your genetic expression. Take the good and leave the rest! Unravel the myths and gather information that you can believe and live from going forward.

Try It Now Writing Exercise #3
What were the values in your family? Some examples might be: hard work; love; spanking; secrecy; substance use; honesty; integrity.

_____
_____
_____
_____
_____
_____
_____

What are the values from your family that you still hold and want to keep?

_____
_____
_____
_____
_____
_____

What are the values you want to let go of?

_____
_____
_____
_____
_____
_____

What is the most important strength you have brought into adulthood from your family?

_____

_____

_____

_____

_____

_____

_____

Try It Now Writing Exercise #4
What was the environment of your family when you were born?

_____

_____

_____

_____

_____

_____

How was love expressed in your family?

_____

_____

_____

_____

_____

**How are you living differently—maybe even better—
because of what you learned in your family?**

_____

_____

_____

_____

_____

_____

_____

**What do you need to do to heal any family relationships
that feel wounded?**

_____

_____

_____

_____

_____

_____

_____

My Daily Practice
  • Try It Now Writing Exercises # 3, #4.

Journal:
  • Journal 15 to 30 minutes.
  • Set one intention for the day that reflects a change you're inviting into your life.
  • Close your eyes and visualize yourself living out this intention. Feel the feeling you would have doing this thing.
  • Happy List: Write about one or more things that went well today. What made you happy? Add it to your "Happy List." Feel the gratefulness throughout your body.

Day 3

Gaining Clarity: Writing My Vision Statements

Vision is the art of seeing the invisible.
– Jonathan Swift

It is time to create your personal vision statements.

Your vision statements will help you keep sight of the bigger picture as you implement changes and take small steps towards transformation. They connect you with your future and are a reminder of the direction you want to go towards in your life. A good vision statement is a living document containing your dreams and aspirations.

Tomorrow we'll spend some time looking at the **Daily Conscious Living Plan**. For now, I invite you to consider each category separately. Remember, you are only going to pick one or two to focus on. Your vision for Relationships will be different to your vision for Health. Writing a separate vision for each category you choose to focus on will help you implement the specific changes you are seeking.

Creating a Vision Statement

It is time to look within. Ask yourself the following questions:
- If I never had to work another day in my life, how would I spend my time?

- What are my passions?
- What do I want to create more time for?
- What are some of the things that are important to me but that are not present in my daily   life?
- What are some things that I might regret missing or might make me feel unfulfilled as I   look back on my life?
- What are some of the things I still want to accomplish?
- What needs to change in order for me to accomplish these things?

Review the Categories

The Daily Conscious Living Plan consists of seven categories:

1. Relationships
2. Money/Finance
3. Spirituality
4. Work/Career/Vocation
5. Play
6. Health
7. Creativity

As you review the categories, ask yourself a few questions that relate to each one. There may be room for transformation in each category. But, for now consider which category seems most urgent to you. You can do this plan and focus on a different category at a later time.

Relationships

Looking forward, what do you want in your romantic life? How about your family and other personal relationships? What would make you feel fulfilled in your relationships? What does a "perfect relationship" look like to you? How do you want your relationships to change? Take time to think about the different relationships in your life.

Money/ Finance

What do you need to make you feel secure? Money can provide freedom to do the things we want in the world, but how money translates to security is different for everyone. There's no right or wrong answer. The important thing is to find your truth. How much savings do you need? What are your sources of income? Do you feel a sense of security in terms of this income? What could you do to increase that security? Give this some thought.

Spirituality

What would you like your inner spiritual life to look like? Our spiritual connection speaks to our relationship to God, to our religious community, and to how we relate to others. Would you like to see changes in this area? As part of my daily conscious living plan, I created time to meditate daily. Try meditating on this category and then writing your answers.

Work/Career/Vocation

Much of our life is spent in our chosen career. Occasionally, we get stuck in a choice that no longer fits us. Think about what you see for yourself in your career future. What lies ahead—a change, promotion, school, a new focus? In my vision statement, I saw myself helping others through counseling and teaching, which later evolved into writing. I went back to school, got my Masters, and pursued this new career path, which better fit my vision of family relationships and gave me the flexibility to work and raise children as a single parent. What changes would you like to see?

Play

Play looks different at every stage of our development. What does the word "fun" look like in your future? Does this include travel, going to the beach or the mountains, hiking or cruising? This is about enjoyment and bringing joy into your life.

Health

How do you live in your body? Do you want to lose weight? Do you want to run a marathon? Do you want to drink more water, eat healthier? After the loss of my husband, I decided that I wanted to be really healthy in order to raise my children and keep up with the demands of single parenting. I created a vision to maintain my health with exercise and good eating habits. What does your body need?

Creativity

There are many types of creativity—writing, gardening, drawing, planning meetings or events, cooking. Creativity can be used in just about every aspect of your life. Think and daydream about the ways you love to use your creativity! This is your time to enjoy! How do you want to spend your creative energy?

Try It Now Writing Exercise #5
Consider each of the seven categories separately. Jot down a few notes about each category.

_____

_____

_____

_____

_____

_____

_____

_____

_____

_____

_____

_____

_____

_____

Decide which categories you would like to focus on. Remember, transformation is an ongoing process. Choose whatever resonates most right now.

_____

_____

_____

_____

_____

_____

Review the words you used to describe your vision for each category. Do they feel accurate and honest? Is there anything you'd like to add or amend?

Here are a few suggestions to keep in mind as you write your vision statements.

1. Emotions are the key to making things happen. Connecting with your vision should give you pleasure.
2. Use simple language. This will make your vision statement easier to remember.
3. Use positive language that evokes emotion.
4. Use action verbs to evoke energy.
5. Include a timeframe in your vision statement. This will help keep you focused.
6. Your vision should include some "stretch."

Example:
Spiritual: Vision Statement
Over the next year I will continue to meditate daily, enrich my spiritual connection with God, and create a life filled with peace and tranquility.

Try It Now Writing Exercise #6
Write your Vision Statement for each category you have chosen to focus on.

Category

_____

_____

Vision Statement

_____

_____

_____

_____

_____

_____

Category

_____

_____

Vision Statement

_____

_____

_____

_____

_____

_____

Category

_____

_____

Vision Statement

_____

_____

_____

_____

_____

_____

My Daily Practice:

· **Try It Now Writing Exercise #5, #6.**
· **Review the things you would like to focus on from the various categories. Do your vision statements address these changes? Remember, this should be a stretch!**

Journal:

· **Journal 15 to 30 minutes.**
· **Set one intention for the day that reflects the changes you are inviting into your life.**
· **Visualize yourself doing this activity. Really feel it!**
· **Happy List: Write about one or more things that went well today. What made you happy or grateful? Close your eyes and feel that good feeling throughout your body.**

Day 4

Creating My Daily Conscious Living Plan

If one advances confidently in the direction of his dreams and endeavors to live the life which he has imagined he will meet with success unexpected in common hours making dreams a reality.
– Henry David Thoreau

Categories

It's time to create your **Daily Conscious Living Plan**. This is about balancing your life in a new way, expanding positive thoughts and feelings, and not focusing on the negative thoughts that have controlled your life in the past. This is about doing **more** of what you really love.

There are seven categories in the Daily Conscious Living Plan.

1. Relationships
2. Money/Finance
3. Spirituality
4. Work/Career/Vocation
5. Play
6. Health
7. Creativity

Step-by-step guide to creating a successful Daily Conscious Living Plan

1. Define your ultimate vision for each category you select.
2. Identify activities that fit into one or more specific categories. Ask yourself how it would

feel to do these activities. These activities should evoke positive thoughts, emotions, and feelings. They should support your vision.

Example:

Category: Health

Vision Statement: "I will maintain better health by eating better, exercising, and becoming more conscious of the way I treat my body."

Activities:

Drink 8 glasses of water a day. (Health)

Take regular breaks. Stretch and stand throughout the day. (Work)

 Do one act of kindness each day for someone. (Relationships)

3. Some of the activities will be things that you already do. Look at increasing the level of that activity. It should be a stretch.
4. In order to re-wire your neural pathways, it is important to repeat the activity daily and experience positive thoughts.
5. If you cannot repeat the activity, write down the barrier (such as negative thoughts or resistance to doing that activity). Identifying the barrier makes you more conscious and better able to move through that barrier.
6. Do the same thing each day for 40 Days.
7. If using the point sheet at the back of the journal feels useful, make forty copies—one for each day. Each day, give yourself **one point per activity** that you accomplish. If you are working on four activities you will get four points if

you accomplish all the activities. Some days you may only do three of your activities and get three points. **Count your points each day.** Notice where you resist and identify the barrier. This is not about winning; it is about becoming more aware, **conscious,** and present, and making simple, ordinary activities become a natural practice.

Remember, it takes twenty-eight days to change a habit, but forty days will make it sustainable. **Think of what a stretch would be for you.** Remember—a stretch is designed to take you out of your comfort zone—taking you to a new edge and pushing through—this is the sweet spot where change happens! Here are some suggestions for each category—or make up your own!

Relationships
· Awareness. Become aware of your actions. Jot down positive/negative interactions.
· Use mindfulness to be present and listen to the people in your life—spouse, significant other, friends, co-workers.
· Engage and make eye contact with each person that crosses your path each day.
· Journal to process a stressful relationship situation before reacting.
· Write about the shifts you see in your relationships.
· Say something nice to at least one person each day—a spouse, friend, co-worker.
· What can you do to improve your environment to enhance your relationships?
· Meditate to ask for guidance in a relationship.
· Identify negative thought patterns about past or current relationships.

46

- Write about what you are grateful for in a relationship each day.
- Do something kind for someone daily.
- Relationships are mirrors for our own lives. Focus on responding rather than reacting.
- What do you fear in a relationship? How can you go through the fear?
- Make time for a relationship.
- Join an activity to meet new people.
- Do an activity to open your heart.

Money/Finance

- Monitor daily spending. What do you want to do differently?
- Identify and take action toward how you want to enhance the lives of others with your resources—spouse, significant others, friends, others.
- Take action toward your saving plan.
- Clarify your attitude and conscious language about money.
- Identify your money fears. Write what is true about them.
- Write about your money values and how your daily actions reflect those beliefs. What needs to shift?
- Reflect on your income and resources. Are the things you are doing in the world reflecting the compensation/pay you expect? What do you love about what you do and the compensation you receive for doing it?
- What do your income/resources provide that you are grateful for?
- Open a dialogue about finances with family.
- What is a small daily action you can take to make yourself feel more prosperous?
- Have you felt victimized by your money situation? What are the daily steps you can take to change that?

Spirituality
- Meditate for 10 minutes a day to begin.
- Journal for 20 minutes a day.
- Write an intention each day.
- Spend some time in complete silence each day.
- Look at the Heartmath exercise on Day 21. Meditate about going into your heart each day and note the changes that happen.
- Write a list of what you are grateful for each day—even the little things that make your day move smoothly.
- Spend some time in nature each day. Note how this shifts you.
- Seek out some type of spiritual inspiration each day. Write about what this brings to your life.
- What are the desires of your heart, your soul? Write about these each day. What could fulfill those desires?
- Write about who/what you need to forgive and take an action—writing, meditating, talking, clearing the air—to do that.

Consider how your values reflect your daily life. Incorporate more actions that reflect your values.

Work/Career/Vocation
- Think about what you aspire to at work and identify the actions you can take toward that for the next forty days.
- How can you improve your work? What is lacking? Write a solution you can work on every day.
- What can you do differently to make your day feel more productive? What can you let go of to help with time management?
- What are you grateful for at your work place?
- Write out a plan each morning or evening for that work

day.

- How can you have more focus at work?
- Work-life balance is important. What could you do differently to intentionally make this more manageable?
- Do not complain about work for forty days
- Do you need a coach to help you be successful? Get one!

Play

- Consciously look for opportunities to smile, laugh, have fun!
- What does play look like for you? Can you fit one small thing in your schedule each day that looks like play?
- What makes you smile or laugh? Identify those things and make an effort to put them in your day.
- Too much play? Think about how you can structure your day to give yourself the reward of play without letting it take over your whole life.
- Identify negative thoughts that sabotage play. Write what is true about those negative thoughts so you can enjoy your play.
- Did play feel venerable as a child? Did it feel sarcastic or hurtful? How could play be different now? Write about how you want to play as an adult.
- Play with animals.

Health

- Exercise at least twice a week. Try to sweat at least once a week.
- Take a break from technology for thirty minutes a day.
- Eat consciously. Think about the types of food you are putting in your body. Eat naturally. Avoid sugar, wheat, dairy, and gluten.
- Stretch your body as much as possible.
- Drink at least eight glasses of water a day.

- Push through and go beyond resistance when you exercise.
- Monitor food intake.
- What healthy foods do you enjoy? Eat more of them.
- Write daily about what health means to you.
- Make small changes in your environment to support where you are at this time in your life.
- Do one act of self care daily. Identify a list of what that could be, and smile as you enjoy taking care of yourself.

Creativity

- There are many types of creativity. Gardening, planting, writing, drawing, cutting out pictures, cooking. Pick one creative thing you want to do daily to enhance your life.
- Take a creative class (pottery, jewelry making, painting) and work daily on the project.
- Create a journal that holds your vision.
- Journal about a new business you want to create.
- Spend time in nature—walk and think.
- Make some creative changes in your home.
- Listen to music and think or write.
- Make a product you want to sell.
- Write the desires of your heart and think about how to manifest them in your life.
- Designate a specific time and day to create and put it on your schedule. It's important to schedule play time!

Make a daily plan, and do your best to stick to it. Watch where you resist.

My Daily Conscious Living Plan:

Category

_____

_____

Activities

_____

_____

_____

_____

_____

_____

_____

Category

_____

_____

Activities

_____

_____

_____

_____

_____

_____

_____

Category

_____

_____

Activities

_____

_____

_____

_____

_____

_____

My Daily Practice:
- Create your Daily Conscious Living Plan.
- Review the things you would like to focus on from the various categories. Do your activities fit your vision statements?

Journal:
- Journal 15 to 30 minutes.
- Set one intention for the day that reflects the changes you are inviting into your life.
- Visualize yourself doing an activity that meets this intention. Really feel it!
- Happy List: Write about one or more things that went well today. What made you happy or grateful? Close your eyes and feel that good feeling throughout your body.

Day 5

Rewiring Me: The Role of Science

Just as trees shed their leaves in winter and renew themselves the mind can shed its prejudices, barriers and renew itself.
– Radha Burnier

Neuroscience: What's the brain got to do with it?
As the famous line of Aristotle goes: "We are what we repeatedly do. Excellence, then, is not an act, but a habit." As we unravel the amazing riddles of science, at the top of the list is a new understanding of neuroscience. Neuroscience has taken a quantum leap in the past few years. Scientists used to believe that the process of cell division, which creates new brain cells, slowed down and stopped altogether by the time we were in our teens. The relatively new science of Neuroplasticity has changed all of that.

Research in Neuroplasticity tells us that we are making new brain cells and new neural connections all the time. Neurogenesis, which is the process of creating new neurons and connections, does not stop in childhood but continues into adulthood. Each time we have a new thought or experience, we make a new neural connection. Over the next forty days, with the help of your **Daily Conscious Living Plan** and this journal, you will be re-wiring your brain, paying attention to your desires, and enjoying your life more.

Current research tells us that the first few years of a child's life are a time of rapid brain growth. At birth, every neuron in the cerebral cortex has an estimated 2,500 synapses. By the age of three, this number has grown to a whopping 15,000 synapses per neuron. The more often a pathway is used, the more sensitive and developed that pathway becomes.

As these pathways develop, the collective group of used pathways becomes a map of how an individual thinks, reasons, and remembers. As we gain new experiences, some connections are strengthened while others are eliminated. This process is known as synaptic pruning. Neurons that are used frequently develop stronger connections and those that are rarely or never used eventually die. By developing new connections and pruning away weak ones, the brain is able to adapt to its changing environment.

Neurons that are not stimulated in these pathways tend to wither away and become unusable. This is the good news for us as we determine what we want to let go of in our lives. As we change negative thoughts, beliefs, and behaviors, the old pathways will simply atrophy. These neuron cells either die or change in ways that render them ineffective.

If pathways are never developed, they never become usable. They can never handle significant electrochemical communication traffic within the brain. Long term non-use of connections between sensory neurons and motor neurons can result in a loss of pathway between the two.

As we introduce new activities into our lives, we increase our brain activity. A primary purpose of education is to stimulate more pathways in the brain so that more neurons are used and those pathways are able to handle additional traffic.

Many of our feelings are activated by the sensory system. Each time an item is stored and cross-referenced in the brain, a new pathway to that item is sensitized. Many people associate a memory with a particular song. Each time that song is heard, the memory is relived. The same can be said of smells. This is also why grief and loss are called a "whole body experience"—they are completely triggered by the sensory system.

In Dr. Rick Hanson's book, *Hardwiring Happiness*, he identifies three steps that help an experience sink into your brain. Step One is taking in the good, like reinforcing good thoughts. Step Two is enriching your experience by staying with it. Step Three is absorbing the experience and allowing it to become a part of you. Dr. Hanson explains that by taking in all aspects of an experience, it prolongs the neural activity and helps build neural structure. Staying with a positive feeling allows those feelings to expand.

These three steps are a key part of how our 40-Day plan builds and strengthen new neural networks. As you decide what you want to focus on, you'll also make choices about what you need to let go of. In considering things to include in your plan, notice your feelings. If you love to exercise, include it in your 40-Day plan. If exercise is already a part of your life, then the neural pathway for it already exists. Your new plan might increase or even diversify your exercise. For example, maybe you'll add strengthening exercises to prepare for climbing a mountain. You might really struggle in the first week or two, but it will become easier and easier as those pathways expand. Increasing your activity by small daily increments, like one extra repetition per day, will make the added activity suddenly seem doable. Eventually it will even seem easy.

The popular pseudo-myth tells us that it takes twenty-one to twenty-eight days to create a new habit or pathway. Since your plan is for forty days, you will actually be reinforcing, almost doubling, the new pathway you are creating. Your new plan will also be creating a lot of positive thoughts and emotions along the way.

Leaping The Gap
The subconscious mind stores ninety-five percent of our programming, which is pretty much in place by age seven. But the subconscious cannot determine whether an experience is real or imaginary, it just runs whatever program it is given.

The conscious mind sits behind the prefrontal cortex and controls only five percent of our behavior. It controls our identity and creates pictures of what we want. As we create new pictures of our desires, thoughts reflecting those emotions are carried along a series of electrical impulses, moving from neuron to neuron, leaping across gaps or synapses. The saying "neurons that fire together wire together" is entirely true! Each time you have the same thought there is less resistance to that synaptic leap. You are carving a new pathway from which to operate.

If we default to the subconscious and go back to our old rote behavior patterns, we reinforce old negative thoughts, emotions, and behavior patterns that no longer serve us. We reinforce those outdated neural pathways.

56

Negative thoughts, emotions, and stress result in negative chemicals exploding into our DNA and cells. Drawing on the DNA research in the science of Heartmath, explained on Day 21, we know that DNA can recoil or expand, depending on the emotion we are feeling. In order to stay connected to the greater quantum field, change behavior, and become a part of the flow, it is important to do things that create positive thoughts, feelings, and emotions. This is what opens us up to Awaken. The most important aspect of changing is the FEELING it evokes in your BODY!

Try It Now Writing Exercise #7
Based on the three steps in Dr. Hanson's book, *Hardwiring Happiness*, try this exercise for activating positive emotion in your neural pathways. Think of something that gives you pleasure. Think and write about including this activity in your Daily Conscious Living Plan.

_____

_____

_____

_____

_____

_____

Close your eyes and see yourself doing this activity. As it becomes a part of your life, how would it feel? REALLY FEEL! Write about how great it would feel to do this.

_____

_____

_____

_____

_____

_____

My Daily Practice
·   Try It Now Writing Exercise #7.
·   Review the categories in the Daily Conscious Living Plan. Are there more things you want to add to your plan? Are there some things you are doing that need more attention, perhaps expanding? Revise your plan today.

Journal:
·   Journal 15-30 minutes.
·   Set one intention for the day that reflects something in your plan.
·   Close your eyes and visualize yourself doing one thing on your plan. Feel the feelings you would have as if you are doing this thing.
·   Happy List: Write about one or more things that went well today. What made you happy? Add it to your "Happy List" and feel the gratefulness throughout your body.

Day 6

Finding Joy: The Role of Science

Every breath we take, every step we make, can be filled with peace, joy and serenity. We need only to be awake, alive in the present moment.
– Thich Nhat Hanh

Positive Brain Results

Studies in neuroscience consistently tell us that experiences and the feelings they evoke in us do matter. This is what Dr. Hanson calls experience-dependent neuroplasticity. Research also tells us that in addition to experiences growing into synapses, they also reach down into our genes, into the atoms and molecules of DNA inside the nuclei of neurons, and change how they operate.

Our experiences leave lasting trails in our brains. Your experiences of happiness, worry, stress, negative thoughts, and anxiety make real changes in your neural networks. Your conscious experiences change your nervous system for better or for worse. In other words, your brain is affected by what your mind continues to focus on.

If you continue to focus on negative thoughts, criticism, worry, and stress, the pathways of your brain will be reactive and vulnerable. You will be prone to anxiety and depressed — reactive instead of responsive. But, if you focus on positive experiences, good events, pleasant feelings, changing those negative thoughts and feelings, over time your brain will take a different shape, one with resilience and strength hardwired into it.

Try It Now Writing Exercise #8
Think about a positive time you remember. Perhaps a time when you felt loved or included. Write about that experience.

_____

_____

_____

_____

_____

_____

_____

What could you focus on today that will generate positive thoughts and feelings?

_____

_____

_____

_____

_____

_____

What kind of experience do you want to have today? Write about that!

_____

_____

_____

_____

_____

Staying with a negative experience is like digging a hole you will never get out of. We have everything to gain by remembering positive experiences, so why do we focus on the negative? Because we have been taught to do so.

As you take in the things you love and desire, and implement them in your 40-Day plan, you are growing and building new neural circuits that will easily take you wherever you want to go!

My Daily Practice
·   Try It Now Writing Exercise #8.
·   Review the categories in the Daily Conscious Living
    Plan. Review your vision statements. Are there things
    that need more attention, perhaps expansion? Revise
    your plan today.

Journal:
·   Journal 15-30 minutes.
·   Set one intention for the day that reflects something in
    your plan.
·   Close your eyes and visualize yourself doing one thing
    on your plan. Feel the feelings you would have as if
    you are doing this thing.
·   Happy List: Write about one or more things that went
    well today or made you happy. Add it to your "Happy
    List" and feel the gratefulness throughout your body.

Day 7

Recreating My Environment: Epigenetics

Our environment, the world in which we live and work, is a mirror of our attitudes and expectations.
– Earl Nightingale

Leading research institutes, such as MD Anderson, are now highlighting and exploring the new field of epigenetics. Epigenetics originated in the 1950s, when an English developmental biologist named Conrad Waddington suggested that something was working on top of the DNA sequence to modulate gene expression.

Waddington's work was then advanced by two scientists named Champagne and Issa, who began investigating whether experiences of a person's environment could trigger genetic changes. This work came to be known as epigenetics, and it suggests that our human development is not completely hardwired into our DNA.

The conclusion from Dr. Issa's lab was that epigenetic changes are biological markers on DNA that modify gene expression without altering the underlying sequence. Researchers have found that environmental factors—such as lifestyle, location, trauma, stress, and even diet—can activate epigenetic changes. Although our genes are mostly hardwired at the moment an egg is fertilized by a sperm, epigenetics suggests that our DNA may be more susceptible to change than was previously thought.

In 1990, a group of Russian physicists, biologists, geneticists, embryologists, and linguists began an intense study of DNA. The research project was directed by Dr. Peter Gariaev, a biophysicist and molecular biologist who is a member of the Russian Academy of Sciences. During their eight-year study, the researchers discovered that our DNA is like a complex, biological, micro-computer chip. Furthermore, that microchip communicates with its environment. Dr. Gariaev found that the basic structure of DNA alkaline pairs is the same as that of human language. The researchers concluded that DNA can be influenced and reprogrammed by the thought waves in our environment.

Epigenetics and the Environment

Research shows us that the genome dynamically responds to the environment. Stress, diet, behavior, toxins, and other factors activate chemical switches that regulate gene expression. In other words, if we are in a stressful situation over a prolonged period of time, such as an abusive relationship or stressful work environment, our genes will express differently than a person who is not exposed to those things.

Different experiences cause the epigenetic profiles of each cell type to increasingly differentiate over time. In the end, hundreds of cell types form, each with a distinct identity and a specialized function. Even in differentiated cells, signals fine-tune cell functions through changes in gene expression. A flexible epigenome allows us to adjust to changes in the world around us and learn from our experiences.

Try It Now Writing Exercise #9
How is your current living environment different from the environment you grew up in?

_____

_____

_____

_____

_____

_____

What is the same?

_____

_____

_____

_____

_____

What do you know needs to change to create a different environment?

_____

_____

_____

_____

_____

My Daily Practice

· Try It Now Writing Exercise #9.
· Review your Daily Conscious Living Plan. Is there one more thing you would like to add to your plan? Write it down.

Journal:

· Journal 15 to 30 minutes.
· Set one intention for the day that reflects an activity that you chose from the Daily Conscious Living Plan today.
· Close your eyes and visualize yourself doing the activities that you have chosen from your plan. Feel the feelings you would have doing these activities.
· Happy List: Write about one or more things that went well today, or made you happy. Your "Happy List" should be getting longer!

Day 8

My New Choices: Epigenetics and Inheritance

It is our choices, Harry, that show what we truly are, far more than our abilities.
– J.K. Rowling

Epigenetics and Inheritance

According to the University of Utah's Genetic Science center, we used to think that when an egg is fertilized, that embryo's epigenome was completely erased and rebuilt from scratch. But they discovered that this isn't completely true. Some epigenetic tags remain in place as genetic information passes from generation to generation, a process called epigenetic inheritance.

Epigenetic inheritance is an unconventional finding. It goes against the idea that inheritance happens only through the DNA code that passes from parent to offspring. It means that a parent's experiences, in the form of epigenetic tags, can also be passed down to future generations. As unconventional as it may be, there is little doubt that epigenetic inheritance is real. In fact, it explains some strange patterns that inheritance geneticists have been observing and puzzling over for decades.

Replicating or Recreating Your Environment?

If you are replicating the environment that you grew up in, what is the impact going to be? How would it serve you to look at the environment you grew up in and think about what really needs to be different? Do you think it's possible?

Consider how your environment affects your thoughts and feelings. The realization that you are not limited or defined by the "problems" that defined your parents or the generations before you, releases some of the ingrained belief that your outcomes must be the same as theirs. Your environment is a huge factor in determining the outcome of your gene expression.

Your choices expand and change as your perception of your environment shifts, which changes your negative thoughts and feelings. The result is that you can make new choices that serve you. You no longer have to feel like you are a victim of your circumstances or upbringing. You can draw from your past, but it does not have to define you.

This new understanding of how our environment affects our DNA helps highlight the importance of making new, clear choices in our daily lives, and the impact those choice make on our destiny and our ability to Awaken.

Try It Now Writing Exercise #10
Negative thoughts are created from our beliefs. For
example, a belief that all of the people in your family are
going to have health problems and be overweight. Can
you identify a family habit or belief that you believe
cannot be changed?

_____

_____

_____

_____

_____

_____

_____

Write about a family habit or belief that might be
holding you back from a job, a relationship, or a dream.

_____

_____

_____

_____

_____

_____

What might be possible for you if you change or let go
of this habit or belief?

_____

_____

_____

_____

_____

_____

One of the beliefs that was handed to me by my family of origin was that if you were not a "stay-at-home Mom" your kids would not thrive. But my husband died when our three children were very young and I went back to work shortly after his death. I knew in my heart that my family's belief was not true. I knew that if I could have some sense of life balance, give my children lots of love and nurturing, and set clear limits—doing the best I could do with what I had—my children would not only thrive, but would learn the great quality of resiliency. I was right.

There were many bumps in the road, but my children made it through to adulthood and we all learned a lot along the way. If my thoughts had *not* reflected my new belief, the story might have had a very different ending—perhaps one of guilt and shame, rather than one of resiliency, trust and love. I had to change my own thoughts and beliefs to construct a new belief system, one that supported what I was doing. This new belief system had to reflect what was actually working in my life.

When we have an experience, our response to the experience records a positive or negative outcome in our subconscious brain. The Universe has a wonderful way of presenting situations to us again so that we can experience something in a new way. That sometimes requires us to change our belief system. When we "let go" and allow ourselves to re-experience something differently, it helps us change negative thoughts and belief systems, allowing us to move forward in a new direction based on new thoughts. It heals old wounds or beliefs and enables us to permanently change our behaviors.

Try It Now Writing Exercise #11
What is a situation that has been presented to you more than one time?

_____

_____

_____

_____

_____

_____

_____

Did you handle that situation the same each time or differently?

_____

_____

_____

_____

_____

_____

_____

How could you handle that situation differently in the future?

_____

_____

_____

_____

_____

_____

_____

My Daily Practice

· Try It Now Writing Exercises #10, #11.
· Review your Daily Conscious Living Plan. Review your vision statements. Are the things you have chosen supporting your vision? Write down any changes you need to implement.
  •

Journal:

· Journal 15 to 30 minutes.
· Set one intention for the day that reflects an activity that you chose from the Daily Conscious Living Plan today.
· Close your eyes and visualize yourself doing the activities that you chose from your plan. Feel the feelings you would have when this is accomplished.
· Happy List: Write about one or more things that went well today, or made you happy. Notice how your "Happy List" is growing!

Day 9

My Beliefs: The Role of Spirit

Spirituality is meant to take us beyond our tribal identity into a domain of awareness that is more universal.
– Deepak Chopra

When I am writing, I can look out my window and see the vast colors of blues, pinks, and purples that paint the sky and provide a backdrop for the brilliant orange setting sun. I overlook a beautiful green park, alive with nature and wildlife. As I work, I realize that we are spinning along in the Universe, traveling around that life-giving sun.

I often think how simply amazing it is that all of this is spinning along together simultaneously—you, me, and millions of other souls on this beautiful planet. I am sure that many of you have had that same thought at certain moments in your life. This is science and spirituality at its best—all mixed up together in a huge mixing bowl—and the result is creation at its finest.

If science is the HOW, then spirituality is the WHY. A grand design helps us work within the laws of the Universe, allowing science and spirituality to work together to keep all of this moving and changing. The same is true for each individual being—body, mind, and spirit work together as a microcosm of the Universe. The integration of science and spirituality is critical if we are to manifest true and lasting change in the habits of our daily lives and have the opportunity to fully Awaken.

I had no real grasp of spirituality until my mid-thirties, when my husband died and I was left with three young children to parent and raise. My family's religious beliefs and training centered around a traditional church. To me, that experience was all about sitting still, being quiet, and obeying all the rules.

With the death of my husband, I had to dig deep to understand what my relationship with the Divine really meant. I do not think that I had ever "felt" the presence of God. In other words, church was carved out for Sunday, not as an everyday part of my life. I had to be thrust out of my conventional box and into the unknown to meet God.

I started journaling and listening. Journaling became a form of prayer for me, I literally talked to the Divine daily, and started to listen to the guidance I received. The guidance would always show up in one form or another. As my relationship deepened with the Divine, I knew I was not in this child-rearing thing alone. There was always a Presence guiding and protecting me and my young family along the way.

Wisdom is the integration of understanding and experience. We are a part of and intimately connected to the natural landscape. The same energy that moves the galaxies and the blossoming of a flower governs birth, death, and experiences that give energy to our inner thoughts, feelings, and beliefs. We need to carefully choose the new habits we want to bring into our lives, so that they support the values we are now embracing rather than the values of seasons past. We are working toward living in the present.

Waking up and becoming conscious and returning to a natural state of balance requires an honest assessment of our lives. Are you doing things that bring you joy? What do you want more of in your life? What are your desires? In order to connect to the greater flow in the Universe or in your personal life, you must become more conscious of your actions in the present. The 40-Day Daily Conscious Living Plan is the place to begin practicing this process.

There are many ways to explore your own truth. What you want to change has to align with your values—that is the work of spirituality. People who have conflicting values develop low self-esteem, depression, and anxiety—the inside and outside are not congruent.

As you take a deeper look at your negative thoughts, emotions, beliefs, and experiences, allow Spirit to guide you as you move through to the truth of who you are becoming and what you want to change.

Try It Now Writing Exercise #12
What spiritual/religious belief systems were you raised with?

_____

_____

_____

_____

_____

_____

_____

Have those beliefs changed for you or are they the same?

_____

_____

_____

_____

_____

_____

_____

What is your current belief/experience about God or spirituality?

_____

_____

_____

_____

_____

_____

Do you feel a sense of certainty about these beliefs or are you still exploring?

_____

_____

_____

_____

_____

_____

_____

What beliefs align with your current values?

_____

_____

_____

_____

_____

_____

_____

My Daily Practice

· Try It Now Writing Exercise #12.
· Review Your Daily Conscious Living Plan. Are you moved to add anything? Is it time to increase the level of what you are doing?

Journal:

· Journal 15 to 30 minutes.
· Set one intention for the day that reflects something you chose from the plan.
· Close your eyes and visualize yourself doing one thing on your plan. Can you feel the feelings you would have doing this thing?
· Happy List: Write about one or more things that went well today or made you happy. Add it to your "Happy List." Feel the gratefulness throughout your body.

Day 10

Finding My Center: Meditation

We need silence to be alone with God, to speak to him, to listen to him, to ponder his words deep in our hearts. We need to be alone with God in silence to be renewed and transformed. Silence gives us a new outlook on life. In it we are filled with the energy of God himself that makes us do all things with joy.
– Mother Teresa

The Power of Meditation

In the Psalms we are told, "Be still and know that I am God." A Buddhist text says, "Like a broken gong, be still and silent. Know the stillness of freedom." Why are stillness and meditation so important?

Meditation is the only way that we can consistently bring our attention to one place—the breath. During meditation, our senses settle down and we experience present awareness without thinking. Meditation is the place of silent space where we connect with Oneness, with God. My meditation teacher uses the breath and chanting Om to help me focus. A meditation teacher is a great help to get you started or deepen your practice.

The first step in meditation is finding a comfortable spot where you will not be disturbed. In the beginning, it is best to do short meditations—no longer than ten to fifteen minutes. Seated meditation is normally the least distracting. The second step is to find something to focus on to quiet the mind. The breath works best and is always available to you. Simply close your eyes and follow your breathing. Some people use a "mantra," which means "mind instrument."

Mantras can calm the mental activity of the brain, empower our intentions, and transport us to higher states of awareness. Mantra sounds of "OM" or "SO HUM" are often used. A common complaint in meditation is the mind drifting off from the mantra, with thoughts intruding. Simply acknowledge the thoughts and go back to the mantra or to your breath. You are putting yourself in a state of non-resistance and cultivating a quiet mind.

Studies have shown that people who meditate are able to rapidly dissolve stress and fatigue. The experience of a regular meditation practice leads to an integration of inner silence into your very being. The union of spirit with matter is the essence of spirituality and the essence of being in the flow. We carry this undisturbed state of expanded consciousness with us in our daily lives.

Meditation is a key to unlocking the subconscious and going into a brain state that can bring new behaviors and new energy into our state of being. When I meditate, I go into a space of oneness with God. My breathing takes over, and I simply try to let my mind go blank. It is my time to listen. I usually try to write before or after I meditate. It is important for me to capture some thoughts before I go blank. You might also find it helpful to write before you meditate, as it helps to download the "monkey mind" that seems to plague us when we become silent.

Try It Now Writing Exercise #13
**Find a quiet place. Use your journal to download any
thoughts that are at the forefront of your mind.**

_____

_____

_____

_____

_____

_____

_____

Now you're ready to begin meditating. Allow fifteen
minutes for this process so that you are not rushed.
Set a timer if necessary. Sit on the floor or a chair in a
comfortable position. Sit in an upright position and gently
close your eyes. Start to breathe in and out. Focus only on
your breath. Breathe in and out a few times. As you breathe
out, start to say the word "OM." Allow yourself to stay in
this relaxed state for five to ten minutes. This time can be
expanded with each sitting. Imagine your consciousness
connecting with the consciousness of the Divine.

**When you are finished meditating, write down an
intention you want to focus on for today. It will not just
stay on the page, it will be carried in your heart.**

_____

_____

_____

_____

_____

_____

My Daily Practice
· Try It Now Writing Exercise #13.
· Review Your Daily Conscious Living Plan. Would you like to add anything?

Journal:
· Journal 15 to 30 minutes.
· Set one intention for the day that reflects something you chose from the plan.
· Close your eyes and visualize yourself doing one thing on your plan. Can you feel the feelings you would have doing this thing?
· Happy List: Write about one or more things that went well today or made you happy. Add it to your "Happy List." Feel the gratefulness throughout your body.

Day 11

Becoming me!
Meditation

The thing about meditation is: You become more and more you.
– David Lynch

Meditation cannot be mastered in one day. It is a lifelong practice that must be cultivated over a period of time. Acknowledging that this is just a beginning, we're going to take the next two days to focus on this important practice.

Meditation is the art of focusing 100% of your attention in one area. The practice comes with a myriad of well-publicized health benefits, including increased concentration, decreased anxiety, and a general feeling of happiness.

Although a great number of people try meditation at some point in their lives, only a small percentage stick with it for the long-term. I hope these tips will help you create a sustainable practice as you cultivate the experience of meditation.

1. Be Still: Set aside specific time (preferably two times a day) to be still.
2. Your Breath: Breathe in and out deeply. This slows the heart rate, relaxes the muscles, focuses the mind, and is an ideal way to begin practice.
3. Big Stretch: Doing some big yoga stretches loosens the muscles and tendons, allowing you to sit (or lie) more comfortably. Additionally,

stretching starts the process of 'going inward' and brings added attention to the body.

4. Purpose: Being engaged in your practice is important. Meditation is an ACTIVE process. Try to focus your attention on a single point or mantra and come back to that point or mantra whenever you notice your mind wandering.

5. Frustration: Being frustrated is a very common thing for beginners. Try to go back to the breath and focus. This happens to everyone. Be gentle with yourself.

6. Body position: Experiment with different types of meditation. Try sitting, lying, eyes open, eyes closed, etc. Try to be comfortable without going to sleep.

7. Body Awareness: Notice your body as a meditative state starts to take hold. Once the mind quiets, focus all of your attention on your feet and then slowly move your way up the body (include your internal organs).

8. Location: Create a sacred space. Try arranging candles and other spiritual paraphernalia to help you feel at ease.

9. Awareness: Awareness of your breath and 'being present' while not meditating is a wonderful way to evolve your meditation habits. Taking a walk and focusing on your breath is a great pathway to developing mindfulness.

10. Peaceful Place: The best way to attain deep relaxation is to have a quiet space. Turn off the phone, unplug noisy objects, and make sure you have a room with some privacy.

Try It Now Writing Exercise #14
Set aside a minimum of 30 minutes. You may not need
all of this time but give yourself the space. Create a
special place to meditate. Try using a meditation tape
if that helps quiet the monkey mind. Before you begin,
think about something you need help with and set an
intention. Write your intention here.

_____

_____

_____

_____

_____

_____

_____

Clear your mind and focus on your breath.

Later in your day, journal about your experience.

_____

_____

_____

_____

_____

_____

_____

My Daily Practice
·   Try It Now Writing Exercise 14
·   Review Your Daily Conscious Living Plan. Review
    your Vision Statements. Do you need to add anything
    else? Are you stretching?

Journal:
·   Journal 15 to 30 minutes.
·   Set one intention for the day that reflects what you
    chose from The Plan.
·   Close your eyes and visualize yourself doing one thing
    on your plan. Can you feel the feelings you would
    have doing this thing?
·   Happy List: Write about one or more things that went
    well today or made you happy. Add it to your 'Happy
    List.' Feel the gratefulness throughout your body.

Day 12

Becoming Present: The Practice of Mindfulness

Walk as if you are kissing the Earth with your feet.
– Thich Nhat Hanh

The practice of Mindfulness began to take hold in the West in the 1980s. Mindfulness is about waking up from an automatic life. Mindfulness is what we are implementing when we make new, conscious choices in our lives. Instead of living by rote and automatic behaviors, mindfulness helps us Awaken, enabling us to make choices and making change possible. In our personal lives, many of us have found that the practice of mindfulness can also contribute to our ability to sustain deeply satisfying relationships.

Studies have shown that mindful awareness improves the capacity of the mind to regulate emotions, improve patterns of thinking, and reduce negativity. Research has also shown that mindfulness can be a significant factor in healing the immune system, lowering stress, and creating a general sense of wellbeing. In addition, mindful awareness may directly shape the activity and growth of the parts of the brain responsible for our relationships, our emotional life, and our ability to focus.

Cultivating a mindfulness practice will enable you to weather the rough spots in your life and fully experience the joyful ones with a new depth.

Try It Now Writing Exercise #14
Pick one thing to be mindful about today. It could be a meal, drinking coffee, taking a walk. Slow down your perception of that experience and take in the details. Was it difficult or easy?

_____

_____

_____

_____

_____

_____

_____

What feelings did it bring up for you?

_____

_____

_____

_____

_____

_____

When was the last time you ate a meal and actually thought about what you were eating?

_____

_____

_____

_____

_____

_____

Is the food you eat good for your body? What kind of energy does it give you?

_____

_____

_____

_____

_____

_____

_____

_____

When you have your next meal, slow down and consider the food you are choosing. Tap into the energy it creates. Write about your experience.

_____

_____

_____

_____

_____

_____

_____

My Daily Practice
· Try It Now Writing Exercise #14.
· Review the Daily Conscious Living Plan. How are you doing? Do you need to add something else?

Journal:
· Journal 15 to 30 minutes.
· Set one intention for the day that reflects something you chose from your plan.
· Close your eyes, really feel with your whole body how it would feel to do this thing. Smile as you see yourself doing it.
· Happy List: Write about one thing that went well today. What made you happy? Put it on your "Happy List." Feel the gratefulness throughout your body.

Day 13

Letting Go: Non-Judgmental Awareness

The present moment is filled with joy and happiness. If you are attentive you will see it.

– Thich Nhat Hanh

Mindfulness is bringing open-hearted, non-judgmental awareness into your daily experiences. It is the ability to stay present to the task at hand without thinking about the past or the future. Stress and anxiety build from the untrue and invented thoughts and stories we live out of. Mindfulness is cultivating the practice of being present to whatever experience the moment brings us. It counteracts avoidance. As we enter into an experience, we connect with our feelings, giving us the ability to practice regulating our emotional responses rather than shutting down.

Mindfulness practices have begun to change healthcare and the impact is enormous. With his Mindfulness-Based Stress Reduction program, meditation expert and MIT medical professor Jon Kabat-Zinn helped bring mindfulness into the world of psychiatry. Research has proven meditation to be an effective, low-cost, side effect-free intervention that reduces anxiety and depression, lowers stress levels, and boosts emotional wellbeing. Mindfulness has even been used in addiction treatment.

"Get out of our heads and learn to experience the world

directly, experientially, without the relentless commentary of our thoughts," Mark G. Williams, John D. Teasdale, Zindel V. Segal and Kabat-Zinn wrote in *The Mindful Way Through Depression: Freeing Yourself From Chronic Unhappiness*. "We might just open ourselves up to the limitless possibilities for happiness that life has to offer us."

The practice of mindfulness is beneficial for people experiencing anxiety, depression, chronic pain, and physical symptoms related to stress or disease. Through mindfulness we can see clearly, accept, and gain freedom from the suffering brought on by our automatic thoughts and assumptions. It helps us experience the joy of being fully present in our lives, learn from difficult times, and open to compassion for ourselves and others.

Learning to have compassion, love ourselves, and feel safe are all important parts of the mindfulness process. The more we cultivate love for ourselves, the more we can love others and shift away from a negative place in our lives. The practice of mindfulness is an essential component of learning to recognize and change negative thoughts, allowing us to let them go.

Mindfulness practice includes mindfulness meditation, also known as insight or vipassana meditation. This cultivates open-hearted awareness of one's present-moment experience. A Loving-Kindness statement I return to is:

May I be free from fear.
May I be free from mental suffering.
May I be free from physical suffering.
May I be at ease.

Try It Now Writing Exercise #16
Write your own loving-kindness statement.

_____

_____

_____

_____

_____

_____

_____

My Daily Practice
· **Try It Now Writing Exercise #16.**
· **Review the Daily Conscious Living Plan. How are you doing? Do you want to add something else? Sometimes adding a mindfulness exercise is a help, and a stretch!**

Journal:
· **Journal 15 to 30 minutes.**
· **Set one intention for the day that reflects something you chose from your plan.**
· **Close your eyes, really feel with your whole body how it would feel to do this thing. Smile as you see yourself doing it.**
· **Happy List: Write about one thing that went well today. What made you happy? Put it on your "Happy List." Feel the gratefulness throughout your body.**

Day 14

Discovering Your Inner Life

Do you have the patience to wait till your mud settles and the water is clear? Can you remain unmoving till the right action arises by itself?
– Lao Tzu

Tens of thousand of thoughts go through our minds every day. Most of them are repetitious. Many of them are untrue.

Humans have thinking bodies. Thoughts are not only contained in our minds, but are carried throughout our cellular beings by the chemicals they create. According to research studies, every thought creates a chemical. As your sensory system responds to certain memories over and over, you recreate the chemical response and reinterpret yourself according to those memories. Writing and journaling can help you unearth this rich inner life, making you aware of repeating patterns.

As you journal and discover your innermost thoughts and feelings, you'll be able to observe your own path. Journaling daily for 10 to 15 minutes can help shift your relationships—both internally and externally. Downloading the thoughts that drive you can help ease or erase a preoccupation, making you more available to show up for your life in the present moment.

A conscious commitment to participate in the creation of your own journey will give you a sense of freedom and accomplishment, grounding you in the direction you are choosing to follow. Journaling will heighten your awareness of your values, behaviors, beliefs, experiences, and subtle movements in your own consciousness. As you clear out obsolete programs and binding beliefs, you'll have a unique opportunity to see the world with fresh eyes.

My relationship with journaling started many years ago. I began to journal out of sheer desperation, reeling from the shock of the death of my young husband. Somewhere deep in my bones I knew that journaling was my salvation. I did not understand why journaling worked so well, but I realized that after journaling I felt clear and had a new perspective, with added focus and energy. I could write things I could not say out loud, especially to anyone else. As with any close relationship, sometimes I despised journaling and sometimes it was my best friend, but I always knew I could count on it.

My experience as a psychotherapist has made it clear to me that journaling offers a way to chip away at the blocks, emotions, and beliefs that hold us captive, unleashing thoughts that lie buried deep within each of us.

Many studies have been conducted on journaling in the past few years. Some of the most notable have been done by James Pennebaker, PhD, a professor and chairman of the Psychology Department at the University of Texas at Austin. Dr. Pennebaker has found that individuals who write about traumatic experiences report more positive moods and fewer illnesses. In addition, he reports improved measures of cellular immune-system function, improved liver enzyme effects among university employees, and fewer visits to the student health center for those writing about painful experiences, suggesting that confronting traumatic experiences is physically beneficial. Writing has also been shown to increase working memory. After people write about difficult events in their lives, they devote less cognitive effort to them, which allows them to be better listeners, both in their personal relationships and at work. Most importantly, writing helps us download the preoccupation of negative thoughts, allowing room for new thoughts to emerge.

Try It Now Writing Exercise # 17
What is a "burning" question that you have been carrying around with you?

_____
_____
_____
_____
_____
_____
_____

Write about a fear that won't let go of you.

_____
_____
_____
_____
_____
_____
_____

My Daily Practice
- Try It Now Writing Exercise 17.
- Review the Daily Conscious Living Plan and your Vision Statements. How are you doing? Do you need to increase what you are doing?

Journal:
- Journal 15 to 30 minutes.
- Set one intention for the day that reflects something from your Plan.
- Close your eyes, feel with your whole body how it would feel to do this thing. Smile as you see yourself doing it. Place your hand on your heart and say Thank You to the Divine for letting this wonderful change come into your life.
- Happy List: Write about one thing that went well today. What made you happy? Put it on your 'Happy List.' Feel the gratefulness throughout your body.

Day 15

Editing my Story

My vision is unfolding…the warrior's approach is to say "yes" to life. "Yea" to it all.
– Joseph Campbell

Journaling offers us the opportunity to rewrite our stories. As necessary as it is to download negative thoughts, it is just as important to re-frame our stories as we move forward. Researchers are studying whether the power of writing—and then rewriting—your personal story can lead to behavioral changes and improve happiness. Studies at Duke University show that students prompted to edit their own narratives about college improved their grade point and were less likely to drop out over the next year.

We all have situations that we weave into stories that are not necessarily true! Living out a story that is not accurate can cause us to live in fear, anxiety, or depression. Many stories are not congruent with our own value system, thus causing a disconnect with the expression of who we really are.

Rewriting a story as we would like it to unfold changes our mindset. Try using a different perspective as you rewrite your story. Look at the situation from 18,000 ft. to gain some distance. Examine it from up close to see the detail. If the situation is ongoing, try looking back on it rather than experiencing it in the present. If it's something from your past, try imagining how you would act and react in the present. What is the outcome you would like to enact? Learn to live with the new story as your reality!

Try It Now Writing Exercise #18
Write about a situation that has been preoccupying your mind.

_____

_____

_____

_____

_____

_____

_____

How has this situation affected your life?

_____

_____

_____

_____

_____

_____

Has the effect been positive or negative?

_____

_____

_____

_____

_____

_____

_____

What do you believe is the truth or core of this situation?

_____

_____

_____

_____

_____

_____

_____

What strengths have you used in the past to deal with difficult situations?

_____

_____

_____

_____

_____

_____

What could be the best possible outcome for this situation? Live out this new story!

_____

_____

_____

_____

_____

_____

My Daily Practice
·   Try It Now Writing Exercise 18.
·   Review the Daily Conscious Living Plan and your Vision Statements. How are you doing? Does anything need revision?

Journal:
·   Journal 15 to 30 minutes.
·   Set one intention for the day that reflects something from your Plan.
·   Close your eyes, feel with your whole body how it would feel to do this thing. Smile as you see yourself doing it. Place your hand on your heart and say Thank You to the Divine for letting this wonderful change come into your life.
·   Happy List: Write about one thing that went well today. What made you happy? Put it on your 'Happy List.' Feel the gratefulness throughout your body.

Day 16

Coming Alive: Setting Intentions

Reach high for stars lie hidden in your soul. Dream deep, for every dream precedes the goal.
– Mother Teresa

Intention setting makes a powerful statement to yourself, the community, and the Universe. Taking the time to get clear about your intention and then releasing that into the world carries a powerful force that becomes visible in your life. Intention sets everything in motion.

I set intentions daily. I close my eyes and go into my heart. Body-centered guided meditation helps me align my mental body, emotional body, and physical body. I listen and write my intentions from my heart and carry them with me from that place. Setting intentions helps quiet the "monkey mind"—they simply give the day a different focus, outlook, and energy.

People often ask me the difference between a goal and an intention. A goal is something you want to achieve. An intention is a way you want to be in the world. It's an internal rather than an external focus.

When I set my own daily intentions, I set some small intentions and some large intentions. Large intentions are reflective of the larger pieces of our life, like work or relationships. It is usually easier to begin by writing a small intention about something that is important to you, something that can be done daily and for which you can see the results. It could be as simple as "be kind to everyone I meet today" or "do a great job at work today." You will be amazed how things will show up in your path to support your intention.

When you journal your intentions, you realize that you have the power to re-program yourself to live out those intentions. The act of writing creates synergy with the Quantum Field. Carry your written intentions with you throughout the day. You may find that your day unfolds in ways that surprise you.

It is time to move forward and understand how we are all supported at this particular time. We need to make these changes to Awaken. It is time to become a part of the "tipping point," individually and collectively, to help society move toward a peaceful and sustainable planet. Howard Thurman, an influential American author and philosopher, issues this challenge to us: "Nurture your mind with great thoughts; to believe in the heroic makes heroes. …Go out and do what makes you come alive, because what the world needs most are people who have come alive."

Try It Now Writing Exercise #19
Write a list of all the things you are ready to let go of.

_____

_____

_____

_____

_____

_____

_____

Now write a list of all the things that call to your heart. What are you ready to embrace? What are your greatest desires?

_____

_____

_____

_____

_____

_____

Create and write down an intention to carry with you today. Keep it with you throughout your day.

_____

_____

_____

_____

_____

_____

What did your day bring? How did your intention play out?

_____

_____

_____

_____

_____

_____

My Daily Practice
- Try It Now Writing Exercise #19.
- Review the Daily Conscious Living Plan and your vision statements. How are you doing? Do you need to change what you are doing? Do you need to stretch a little more?

Journal:
- Journal 15 to 30 minutes.
- Set one intention for the day that reflects something from your plan.
- Close your eyes, feel with your whole body how it would feel to do this thing. Smile as you see yourself doing it. Place your hand on your heart and say Thank You to the Divine for letting this wonderful change come into your life. Feel your gratitude!
- Happy List: Write about one thing that went well today. What made you happy? Put it on your "Happy List." Feel the gratefulness throughout your body.

Day 17

My Focus: Intention Setting

Our intention creates our reality.
– Wayne Dyer

As we learn to create and live out of new intentions, we find we can no longer live out of our old beliefs, negative thoughts, or old stories. When an intention is written clearly over and over, the solution starts to present itself. The mind is trained to focus on finding the solution. In Deepak Chopra's book, *Ageless Body, Timeless Mind*, he states that "An intention is a signal sent from you to the field, and the result you get back from the field is the highest fulfillment that can be delivered to your particular nervous system."

Intention is one of the most powerful tools we have at our disposal. It is a conscious force that starts a chain of events, beginning in our brain with the reprogramming of our own neural pathways, and connecting us with the greater Quantum Field. Repetition is an important part of reprogramming the brain. That is why writing our intentions over and over again is important.

The following are some tips for writing a good intention:
· Write the intention with clarity.
· Be specific about what you want, include as much detail as possible.
· Expect results.
· Keep track of your results.
· Think of other times in your life when you have gotten

results.
- "Let go." Know that the highest fulfillment possible is in motion.
- Visualize and feel what it will be like when your intention manifests.
- Rewrite your intention every day until you see results of some kind.
- Journal about the results you receive.
- Practice gratefulness.
- Write small intentions and large intentions.

Try It Now Writing Exercise #20
Write one intention that is small. For example, "I am going to be kind to everyone I meet today." Stay mindful of your intention throughout the day.

_____
_____
_____
_____
_____
_____
_____

Write one large intention. For example, "It is my intention to bring great books into the world, to share knowledge, and help others to heal." Stay mindful of your intention throughout the day.

_____
_____
_____
_____
_____
_____
_____

My Daily Practice
· Try It Now Writing Exercise #20.
· Review the Daily Conscious Living Plan and your vision statements. How are you doing? Does anything need revision?

Journal:
· Journal 15 to 30 minutes.
· Set one intention for the day that reflects something from your plan.
· Close your eyes, feel with your whole body how it would feel to do this thing. Smile as you see yourself doing it. Place your hand on your heart and say Thank you to the Divine for letting this wonderful change come into your life.
· Happy List: Write about one thing that went well today or made you happy. Put it on your "Happy List." Feel the gratefulness throughout your body.

Day 18

My Intuition: How Does Your Life Reflect the Grand Design?

Your vision will become clear only when you can look into your own heart. Who looks outside, dreams; who looks inside, awakens.
– Carl Jung

As we consider what we want to change in our lives, we are really talking about expanding our lives, extending who we currently are to who we want to become as a new possibility in the Universe. As we strive to understand how every part of the Universe is connected, we as humans are discovering what it means to be connected, not only to each other, but also to nature and the Universe. Our physical selves and our emotional inner lives are connected to the greater energetic field of the Universe.

Experiments in Neuroscience, Heartmath, Epigenetics, Fractal Energy, and Quantum Physics tell us that the inner world of our emotions, thoughts, and feelings really do have an effect on what is happening around us. This awareness highlights once more how negative thoughts and feelings can impact each experience we have, how we are connected to others, and how we will continue to generate more of the same experiences if we do not become more conscious in our thoughts and actions. If negative thoughts do not change, they can become a barrier that blocks our ability to penetrate or connect to the greater field of what we desire.

Each person's mind contributes to the collective whole. It has been suggested that we are all connected though consciousness. A story I heard at a conference had a profound impact on me and really illustrates this point. A woman at the conference said that she was from New York and lived close to the site of Ground Zero. After months of helping with the clean up after 9/11, she realized that she herself needed to heal. She scheduled a trip to Costa Rica to see a friend. While in Costa Rica her friend arranged for her to meet with the Indigenous people. A guide took them far back into the jungle. After a couple of days of travel into the depth of the forest, they arrived at the camp of the Indigenous people. She was introduced to the King of the tribe. With the help of a translator, the King told her about a vision he had that a great wound had been done to the United States. He said the great wound had caused much suffering and had created a hole in the earth. She was shocked and amazed that this man knew of 9/11 without any means of communication with the outside world. This is but one of many accounts of how Indigenous people have communicated throughout the years.

It is important to consider not only how the changes you choose to make will affect you personally, but ultimately how these changes affect the connections you have with others and the world around you. If a change on any level affects the whole, each of us changing individually can make a huge difference in our collective reality and to the world that surrounds us.

I have had experiences where I think I am doing something for one reason, but the outcome and experience is far different from my original intention. It is as if "unseen hands" are guiding that experience and many more possibilities open to me. One particular experience stands out. Many years ago, I went on what I thought was going to be a fun trip to Colorado to visit a friend. I was in the midst of writing a book and simply could not finish it. The book needed a good ending and, as much as I tried, it just was not happening. I left for my trip, and even though I had put the manuscript aside, thoughts about the ending kept bubbling up. Little did I realize at the time that my subconscious was still focusing on finding "the perfect ending."

I had several amazing spiritual experiences on this trip. These experiences became exactly what I needed to give the book that rich, savory ending it deserved. I did not look for the experiences, they simply came into my path because I was open and did not try to "force" the ending to unfold in a certain manner. I believe that the inner world of my thoughts helped to orchestrate the chain of events and experiences—science and spirituality coming together to bring the exact experiences I needed into my path. It was pretty cool! When we don't force something to happen, the perfect pieces can be put into place.

Try It Now Writing Exercise #21
As we use our intuition it becomes stronger and stronger. When have you had a situation that involved a knowing, an insight or intuition that you did or did not act upon?

_____
_____
_____
_____
_____
_____
_____

What did you learn from that situation?

_____
_____
_____
_____
_____
_____

Try It Now Writing Exercise #22
What is a decision that you have made that has had a completely different outcome than you expected? Like the decision had a life of its own?

_____
_____
_____
_____
_____
_____

What drove that decision? Did it come from fear or intuition?

_____

_____

_____

_____

_____

_____

_____

_____

What was the outcome?

_____

_____

_____

_____

_____

_____

_____

_____

As we move forward to open our minds to the many possibilities of how we are connected to the world around us, my hope is that you will see the weaving of a perfect cloth for yourself—a cloth alive with many different strands, representing the generative ability of both science and spirit to provide the perfect wardrobe for you to choose from in this life path.

My Daily Practice
- Try It Now Writing Exercises #21, #22.
- Review your Daily Conscious Living Plan. Chart your experience meeting resistance and identifying successes.

Journal:
- Journal 15 to 30 minutes.
- Set one intention for the day that reflects something from your plan.
- Close your eyes, feel with your whole body how it would feel to do this thing you have written about. Smile as you see yourself doing it. Place your hand on your heart and say Thank You to the Divine for letting this wonderful change come into your life.
- Happy List: By now your list should be getting really long!! Write about one or more things that went well today. Put it on your "Happy List." Feel the gratefulness throughout your body.

Day 19

Connecting with Nature: The Role of Science

The goal of life it to make your heartbeat match the beat of the universe. To match your nature with nature.
– Joseph Campbell

Fractal Geometry
In exploring the role of science to determine the similarities we share with nature, I became aware of the book *The Fractal Geometry of Nature,* by Franco-American mathematician Benoît Mandelbrot. In this book, Mandelbrot highlights the many occurrences of fractal objects in nature. Mandelbrot coined the word "fractal," derived from the Latin adjective fractus, to denote anything that is like a broken up stone—irregular and fragmented.

Mandelbrot began to identify fractals throughout almost every facet of our society. One example he gives is a wireless antenna. They began as sticks, then the shape started to evolve in fractals. Fractal-based antennas pick up the widest range of known frequencies and are now used in many wireless devices. Another example he gives is concrete. The concrete used by Ancient Romans was impermeable. Water dissolved it and chunks of it would fall off. At a conference Mandelbrot attended, a speaker introduced an altogether new kind of concrete that is enormously stronger and more durable—a form based entirely on his deep understanding of fractals. Another basic example he gave was a tree. Each split in a tree from trunk to limb to branch is remarkably similar, but with subtle differences that provide increasing detail, complexity, and insight into the inner workings of the tree as a whole.

Fractal patterns appear in almost all of the physiological processes within our bodies. Originally the human heart was believed to beat in a regular, linear fashion, but recent studies have shown that the true rhythm of a healthy heart fluctuates radically in a distinctively fractal pattern. Blood is also distributed throughout the body in a fractal manner. Biology and healthcare are only some of the latest applications of fractal geometry.

The developments arising from the Mandelbrot set are as diverse as the alluring shapes it generates. Even computer-based graphic design and image editing programs use fractals to create beautiful images and effects.

Why is this information important for us to know? Because it tells us that fractal patterns are, as Mandelbrot describes it, the "geometry of the cosmos." Fractal patterns help us to be aware that, once again, the blueprint of our lives, our patterns, are crossing over into science. It highlights how the grand design of everything is connected, not only in our individual lives, but in nature as well.

In light of this deep structural connection, it is not surprising that human beings feel such a strong connection to nature. An article about mindfulness published in the *Huffington Post* in 2013 highlights the value of this connection. Arianna Huffington asked, "In our culture of overwork, burnout, and exhaustion, in which we're connected and distracted 24/7 from most things that are truly important in our lives, how do we tap into our creativity, our wisdom, our capacity for wonder, our wellbeing and our ability to connect with what we really value?"

Her answer was something called "Solvitur ambulando," which is Greek for "it is solved by walking." Mindful people know that simply going for a walk can be an excellent way to calm the mind, gain new perspective, and facilitate greater awareness. According to a 2013 study conducted in the UK, walking through green spaces may actually put the brain into a meditative state. The act of walking in a peaceful outdoor landscape was found to trigger "involuntary attention," meaning that the person walking could hold attention and focus while also allowing for reflection.

Try It Now Writing Exercise #23
When have you felt a strong connection to nature?

_____
_____
_____
_____
_____
_____
_____

What were you doing? Where were you? Describe the place and how it felt.

_____
_____
_____
_____

_____

_____

_____

How do you connect with nature daily?

_____

_____

_____

_____

_____

_____

_____

How do you feel when you connect with nature?

_____

_____

_____

_____

_____

_____

_____

My Daily Practice

· Try It Now Writing Exercise #23.
· Review your vision for the categories you picked. Are you heading toward your vision? Do you need to add or change any steps? Repetition of the steps you have created is very important.

Journal:

· Journal 15 to 30 minutes.
· Set one intention for the day that reflects what you chose from the Daily Conscious Living Plan.
· Close your eyes. Take a deep breath. Visualize yourself accomplishing one of the things on your plan.
· Happy List: Write about one thing, or more that one thing, that went well today. What made you happy? What made you smile? Describe this thing. Add it to your "Happy List."

Day 20

Energy Connections: Quantum physics

We are all connected; To each other, biologically, to the earth, chemically. To the rest of the universe automatically.
– Neil deGrasse Tyson

The conversation about who we are would not be complete without a discussion of quantum physics. Quantum physics tells us that we are connected by waves and particles of atoms, light, and energy. Our thoughts, feelings and beliefs directly affect everything around us, including our consciousness. Furthermore, it is not only our own consciousness affecting the quantum field, every person on the planet affects that field.

Your thoughts, negative or positive, affect the consciousness of the planet. Did you know you were that powerful? This is an important part of our conversation as we grapple to understand how our lives and actions collectively fit into the grand design.

Quantum Possibilities

Let's get a little background on quantum physics here. Einstein's scientific contributions revolutionized almost every aspect of modern physics, including quantum theory. He redefined the core concepts of space and time in which physical events take place and the objective reality in quantum systems.

In 1927, Werner Heisenberg and Niels Bohr from the

Institute for Theoretical Physics in Copenhagen, Denmark, made remarkable discoveries about the quantum structure of matter. Their theory, the Copenhagen Interpretation, states that the universe exists as an infinite number of overlapping possibilities.

In Lynne McTaggert's book, *The Bond*, she explains, "Heisenberg discovered that all subatomic particles do not remain the same at any moment. He says that these particles are constantly trading information with their environment and being reshuffled in a dynamic pattern. The universe contains an indeterminate number of vibrating packets of energy that constantly pass energy back and forth as if in an endless game of basketball with a quantum sea of light."

In other words, our world is a soup of possibilities. Eventually, something happens to lock one of the possibilities into place. That something can be as simple as a thought or act of awareness. The way we see something can convert a quantum possibility into reality. I have even heard quantum physics referred to as "quantum possibilities."

In Greg Braden's book, *The Divine Matrix*, he writes, "both science and mysticism describe a force that connects everything together and gives us the power to influence how matter behaves, and reality itself, simply through the way we perceive the world around us."

Braden urges his readers to consider the Penrose Interpretation, which states that quantum possibilities are a form of matter. Braden explains that because all matter creates gravity, each possibility has its own gravitational field. It takes energy to maintain this field, and the more energy a probability requires, the more unstable it becomes. Because it's impossible to sustain enough energy to keep all of the possibilities going forever, eventually they collapse into a single state—the most stable one, which we see as our 'reality.'

Making a Quantum Shift

In the film *The Shift*, Dr. Wayne Dyer identifies four qualities involved in making a "quantum shift or leap." The first is that it is vivid, we can clearly see that something is changing. The second is surprise, something we were not expecting happens. The third is that it is benevolent, it feels good. And the fourth is that it is enduring, it has God within it. In a quantum shift, we let go of control and allow our Source or God to direct the show.

When we learn to listen, focus, and become fully present, we communicate in new ways that affect the quantum particles. Identifying and shifting our own negative thoughts and beliefs is key to changing paradigms that block us or no longer serve us. This is how we gain access to new choices.

The negative 'tapes' that we play again and again in our minds block our ability to access what we need to attract from the quantum field. I think of negative thoughts as a barrier, like a fence with no gate, prohibiting us from gaining access to the next place in our lives. In other words, we are limiting our own choices, keeping ourselves in the same box and wondering why things don't change.

So, how do we change this thought process? When a negative thought arises, try to name the real truth about that thought. When we know the truth, the negative thought loses its power over us. Changing the negative thought to a positive one creates that gate opening to a whole new field of possibilities.

I had a client who had a negative thought so ingrained in her she had to monitor it daily, sometimes hourly! It started to affect everything she was involved in. She was stuck on a repetition of, "Everyone has more than I do. I will never have what they have." Her family had programmed the thought into her over many years and it now bombarded her in every situation: work; social settings; and in regards to her finances. When she was invited to a function the relentless thought crept in as she looked around the room. She found herself saying, "She has more than me. I will never have what she has." As she became aware of this negative mantra, and the untruth of the statement, she started to change this negative process. Every time the negative mantra popped up, she actively worked to change it. At the next function she was invited to, she said, "I am so glad to be included in this function. It is so fun to be around like-minded, interesting people." Gradually her world started unfolding in a different way, with new opportunities and new avenues of prosperity.

As we observe ourselves making new conscious choices, we become aware of the tremendous possibilities that could exist not just for ourselves, but for everyone.

Try It Now Writing Exercise: #24
Are you aware of your negative thoughts?

_____
_____
_____
_____
_____
_____
_____

What is a negative thought mantra that is keeping you stuck?

_____
_____
_____
_____
_____
_____
_____

What is the truth about that negative thought?

_____
_____
_____
_____
_____
_____

How do negative thoughts, feelings and beliefs affect you and how you interact with the world?

_____

_____

_____

_____

_____

_____

How do these negative thoughts keep you in a negative spiral or block you from what you want in life?

_____

_____

_____

_____

_____

_____

How has your negative situation been a teacher?

_____

_____

_____

_____

_____

_____

The next time this negative thought arises, take the opportunity to change the negative thought to a positive one. Brainstorm some possibilities now.

_____

_____

_____

_____

_____

_____

_____

Try It Now Writing Exercise # 25
Explore the full range of possibilities that are available to you. What are a few possibilities that you have considered, even though they seem 'unreachable'?

_____

_____

_____

_____

_____

_____

Can you form a picture of one of those possibilities and what it would be like to live it?

_____

_____

_____

_____

_____

_____

Spend about 15 minutes a day thinking and writing about that possibility in detail. What would it feel like if this amazing possibility came true? Take 15 minutes now, and then write about your experience.

_____

_____

_____

_____

_____

My Daily Practice:

· Try It Now Writing Exercises 24, 25.
· Review your Daily Conscious Living Plan. Is there one more thing you would like to add? Write it down.
  •

Journal:

· Journal 15 to 30 minutes.
· Set one intention for the day that reflects an activity that you choose from the Daily Conscious Living Plan today.
· Close your eyes and visualize yourself doing the activity you chose from your plan. Feel the feelings you will have when this is accomplished.
· Happy List: Write about one or more things that went well today, or made you happy. Your 'Happy List' should be growing!

Day 21

Heart Energy: HeartMath

My Heart is open. I allow the Universe to guide me through my thoughts, my intuition, my feelings and my encounters. I am fully open to receive the guidance and to follow it.
— Elena Stasik

Our bodies are electrical in nature. If you rub your hands together you feel electricity. When you shuffle your feet across a rug and then touch something you get a small shock. Our hearts contain biological electrical circuits and we can measure the electrical activity by using a electrocardiograph (EKG).

As we continue to explore research that can impact changes in our thoughts, feelings, and emotions, the study of HeartMath offers important information and techniques. For centuries, the heart has been considered the source of emotion, courage, and wisdom. At the Institute of HeartMath (IHM) Research Center in Boulder Creek, California they are exploring the physiological mechanisms by which the heart communicates with the brain, thereby influencing information processing, perceptions, emotions, and health.

HeartMath asks questions such as: Why do people experience the feeling or sensation of love and other positive emotional states in the area of the heart and what are the physiological ramifications of these emotions? How do stress and different emotional states affect the autonomic nervous system, the hormonal and immune systems, the heart and brain?

HeartMath researchers have experimented with different psychological and physiological measures, but it is consistently heart rate variability, or heart rhythms, that stand out as the most dynamic and reflective of inner emotional states and stress. It has become clear that negative emotions lead to increased disorder in the heart's rhythms and in the autonomic nervous system, thereby adversely affecting the rest of the body. In contrast, positive emotions create increased harmony and coherence in heart rhythms and improve the balance in the nervous system.

Researchers have observed that the heart acts as though it has a mind of its own and profoundly influences the way we perceive and respond to the world. In essence, it appears that the heart affects intelligence and awareness. Hearthmath provides a scientific basis to explain how and why the heart affects mental clarity, creativity, and emotional stability.

So, if we are living in an environment of fear, instability, or negativity, what is that doing to our ability to live, love, work, and play in a way that supports the better choices we are attempting to make in our lives? The question then becomes, how can we make choices that nurture the positive qualities we want to infuse in our lives? What needs to change?

I had a client with a very stressful job. When his stomach started to hurt before work every day, he realized that he had to make a change. He knew he could not just walk out and leave his job—he had to make a living. So he started to make other changes to improve his life. He started running in the morning before work, connecting with nature in a new way. He began taking more breaks during the day. He became more mindful of his conversations at and about work—he consciously stopped complaining. He changed his food intake at work, which had been more junk than anything else, and started to eat good food, vegetables, fruits, and water.

As his focus shifted to self-improvement, he became calmer and more able to handle the workload. He no longer resented being at work. He was rewiring internally—mentally and physically. Within a few months of starting his new regime, a more lucrative position became available within the company, so he applied for the job and eventually got it. As he changed internally, everything changed externally.

Try It Now Writing Exercise #26
Write about an experience in which you experienced stress in your body as well as emotionally.

_____

_____

_____

_____

_____

_____

What did your body feel like?

_____

_____

_____

_____

_____

_____

What did you do to get out of that stressful feeling?

_____

_____

_____

_____

_____

_____

My Daily Practice
· Try It Now Writing Exercise #26.
· Review the Daily Conscious Living Plan. Look at your vision statements. Review the things you are focusing on in each category. Can you stretch a little more?

Journal:
· Journal 15 to 30 minutes.
· Set one intention for the day that reflects something you chose from the Daily Conscious Living Plan.
· Close your eyes and visualize yourself doing this one thing on your plan. Really feel it!
· Happy List: Write about one or more things that went well today. What made you happy? Add it to your "Happy List."

Day 22

My Power Center: Thinking vs. Feeling

True creativity quite simply starts with balancing your emotions and activating the power of the heart. Through practicing emotional management from the heart, you tap into the highest form of creativity possible—recreating your perceptions of reality.
– Doc Childre

What makes the heart so important and powerful? Dating back to the Ancient Greeks, human thinking and feeling, or intellect and emotion, were always considered separate functions. In fact, the Greeks called them contrasting aspects of the soul. HeartMath research demonstrates that tools and techniques designed to increase coherence in the emotional system can often bring the mind into greater coherence as well.

HeartMath is finding that the degree of coherence between the mind and emotions can vary considerably. When they are out-of-phase, overall awareness is reduced. Conversely, when they are in-phase, awareness is expanded. This interaction affects us on a number of levels: vision; listening abilities; reaction times; and mental clarity. Grief and loss is a great example of this. After a significant loss one feels confusion, low energy, and an inability to concentrate. This is why grief is called "a whole body experience."

HeartMath researchers have found that prolonged positive emotions, such as love, compassion, and happiness, are associated with coherent heart rhythm patterns. Using measurement devices such as Electrocardiograms and Magnetocardiograms, researchers have discovered a direct connection between heart rate rhythms and the electromagnetic field of the human body, demonstrating that physiological patterns can be encoded directly into our heart's electromagnetic field. This connection is important because the heart exhibits the most powerful electromagnetic field of any organ in the body, a field five thousand times greater than that of the brain. Data from the Institute of HeartMath shows that the heart's electromagnetic field becomes increasingly organized during uplifting emotional heart-coherent states.

This revolutionary research continues thanks to programs such as Princeton University's Princeton Engineering Anomalies Research program (PEAR). For over thirty years, Princeton researchers performed millions of trials studying the effects of human intention. One of PEAR's most notable studies, conducted by Dr. Robert Jahn, demonstrates that frustration and anger actually shut down our ability to remotely influence our surroundings. On the other hand, surrender and love increase our capacity to remotely influence the world around us.

In 1992, IHM chose to focus its research on measuring the effects of human emotions on DNA. The experiments began by isolating human DNA in a glass beaker and then exposing it to a powerful form of feeling known as "coherent emotion." The participants intentionally quieted the mind, shifted their awareness to the heart area, and focused on positive emotions. After performing a series of tests to analyze the test DNA—both chemically and visually—the implications were undeniable. Human emotion changed the shape of the DNA. Without physically touching it or doing anything other than creating specific feelings in their bodies, participants were able to influence the DNA molecules in the beaker. According to one researcher, "the experiments revealed that different intentions produced different effects on the DNA molecule causing it to either wind or unwind," depending on the emotion.

Just like cleaning out your closets and getting rid of old clothes, changing your negative thoughts, feelings, and beliefs makes room for new conscious choices and habits in your life. This change requires that you let go of old habits. Letting go has to be intentional.

Try It Now Writing Exercise #27
How was love expressed in the family you grew up in?

_____

_____

_____

_____

_____

_____

_____

What other feelings and emotions were expressed in your family?

_____

_____

_____

_____

_____

_____

_____

How do you currently express love to the people in your life?

_____

_____

_____

_____

_____

_____

How is it different from the way in which love was expressed in the family you grew up in?

_____

_____

_____

_____

_____

_____

Try It Now Writing Exercise #28
Close your eyes and put your hand on your heart. See
yourself as a young child. Tell that child how much
you love them and send that young child love from
your heart. Tell that child you will take care of them
and never allow them to be harmed. Do this every day
for at least a month. This practice changes your cell
chemistry and activates your heart chakra. What did
you experience when you tried this today?

_____

_____

_____

_____

_____

_____

_____

What loving thoughts can you focus on today?

_____

_____

_____

_____

_____

_____

**Gratitude is a good place to start. Write a list of some of
the things and people you are grateful for today.**

_____

_____

_____

_____

_____

My Daily Practice
·   Try It Now Writing Exercises #27, #28.
·   Review the Daily Conscious Living Plan. Review your
    vision statements and the things you are focusing on
    in each category.

Journal:
·   Journal 15 to 30 minutes.
·   Set one intention for the day that reflects something
    you chose from the Daily Conscious Living Plan.
·   Close your eyes and visualize yourself doing this one
    thing on your plan. Really feel it!
·   Happy List: Write about one or more things that went
    well today. What made you happy? Add it to your
    "Happy List."

Day 23

My Emotional Connections: DNA Research and Experiments

Out beyond our ideas of wrongdoing and right doing there is a field, I will meet you there.
– Rumi

Research continues to show that human emotion, positive or negative, has a large influence on the way our cells function in our body. In Gregg Braden's book, *The Divine Matrix*, he cites a 1992 study reported in the journal *Advances.* In the study, a US Army scientist investigated whether or not the power of our feelings continues to have an effect on living cells, specifically DNA, once those cells are no longer part of the body.

The researchers started by collecting a swab of tissue and DNA from the inside of a volunteer's mouth. This sample was then isolated and taken to another room in the same building, where they began to investigate a phenomenon that modern science says should not exist. In a specially designed chamber, the DNA was measured electrically to see if it responded to the emotions of the donor, who was in another room a few hundred meters away.

The donor was shown a series of video images designed to create genuine states of emotion inside the body. The material ranged from graphic wartime footage to erotic images to comedy. The idea was for the donor to experience a spectrum of real emotions within a brief period of time.

When the donor experienced emotional "peaks" and "dips," his cells and DNA showed powerful electrical response at the same moment in time. Although the donor and the sample were in different rooms and a few hundred meters apart, the DNA acted as if it was still physically connected to the person's body.

The US Army discontinued its experiment; however, one of the researchers continued. The new experiments introduced greater distances—up to 350 miles (560 km) between the donor and the DNA sample. The time lapse between the donor's experience and the cells' response was gauged by an atomic clock located in Colorado. In each experiment, the interval measured between the emotion experienced by the donor and the cells' response was zero, the effect was simultaneous! Whether the cells were in the same room or separated by hundreds of miles, the results were the same. When the donor had an emotional experience, the DNA reacted as if it were still connected to the donor's body.

While this may sound quite weird, consider what it means. There must be some sort of a connecting field linking all matter. That is, everything must be— and must remain— connected. As one of the researchers said, "There is no place where one's body actually ends and no place where it begins."

These studies are startling. We frequently hear stories of organ recipients who take on the feelings of their donor. In light of this research, those stories make more sense. I hear stories every day about how parents intuitively "know" when something is going on with their children. Perhaps most importantly, this study reveals the enormous effect our thoughts and emotions have on our DNA—and on the energy fields surrounding us.

Try It Now Writing Exercise #29
What is the emotion you feel most often? Is it positive or negative?

_____

_____

_____

_____

_____

_____

_____

What triggers that emotion?

_____

_____

_____

_____

_____

_____

If the emotion is negative, how could you change your response to become positive?

_____

_____

_____

_____

_____

_____

_____

What would you have to let go of in order to experience positive emotions?

_____

_____

_____

_____

_____

_____

_____

My Daily Practice
·   **Try It Now Writing Exercise #29.**
·   **Review the Daily Conscious Living Plan. Review the things you are focusing on in each category of the plan.**

Journal:
·   **Journal 15 to 30 minutes.**
·   **Set one intention for the day that reflects something you chose from the Daily Conscious Living Plan**
·   **Close your eyes and visualize yourself doing this one thing on your plan. Really feel it!**
·   **Happy List: Write about one or more things that went well today. What made you happy? Add it to your "Happy List."**

Day 24

Tipping Points: The Role of Spirit

*The void is where God is…God is the potential fullness gushing
out from every empty space, the ever present possibility of a
magic moment or a miraculous thought. Off the blank page
jumps a cosmic summons, out of the silence came the opening of
Beethoven's Fifth. We must embrace the void instead of resisting it.
That is the way of the mystic. It is the only way we can heal.*
– Marianne Williamson

We look to our spiritual masters to give us insight into
paradigm shifts that have taken place across many
lifetimes. These spiritual teachers have chosen to live
differently and, in doing so, have offered us new and
different blueprints from which to operate. The world
has been changed by those with a gentle spirit and inner
strength.

Martin Luther King, Jr., Gandhi, Buddha, Jesus Christ,
Mother Teresa, Lao Tzu, and Mohammed all lived in a new
way, offering a paradigm shift within the specific cultures
they were born into. The seeding of these new ideas shows
how existing cultures can begin to shift based on the beliefs
and work of a single individual. While these spiritual
masters were among the first to accomplish this, they will
certainly not be the last. Drawing on what we know about
how thoughts affect consciousness, it takes relatively few
people to create a greater shift.

In his book *The Tipping Point,* Malcolm Gladwell points
out that ideas, products, messages, and behaviors spread

like viruses. As we change our negative thoughts, feelings, and beliefs, we have an opportunity to anchor ourselves and others in a new reality. Gladwell highlights three characteristics: contagiousness; little causes that can have big effects; and change that happens not gradually but at one dramatic moment. The name he gives to the dramatic moment in an epidemic when everything can change all at once is the Tipping Point. Common examples include how measles moves through a grade school and how when someone yawns it can set off others around them.

Tipping Points have wider sociological implications as well. Gladwell cites some examples taken from the work of Jonathan Crane, a sociologist at the University of Illinois, who looked at the effect "high status" role models (managers, professionals, and teachers) had on the lives of teenagers in their neighborhoods. He found little difference in the pregnancy rates or school dropout rates in neighborhoods that had forty to fifty percent high status workers. But when the number of professionals dropped below five percent, problems exploded.

Like the spiritual masters, we can be a part of the positive Tipping Point not only for ourselves, but for the world around us.

Try It Now Writing Exercise #30
When have you experienced a situation where the beliefs of one person influenced the people around you in a good way?

_____

_____

_____

_____

_____

_____

When have you experienced a situation where the beliefs of one person influenced the people around you in a negative way?

_____

_____

_____

_____

_____

_____

Have you ever experienced a "Tipping Point" in your own life?

_____

_____

_____

_____

_____

_____

My Daily Practice
- Try It Now Writing Exercise #30.
- Review the Daily Conscious Living Plan. Review your vision statements in the categories you chose. Look over the things you are focusing on in each category.

Journal:
- Journal 15 to 30 minutes.
- Set one intention for the day that reflects something you chose from the Daily Conscious Living Plan.
- Get a visual. Print or draw a picture if possible. Close your eyes and visualize yourself doing this one thing on your Plan. Really feel it!
- Happy List: Write about one or more things that went well today. What made you happy? Add it to your "Happy List." Wow!! This list is getting long—are there some repeats?

Day 25

My Beliefs: Comparing Science and the Spiritual Masters

At this moment you are seamlessly flowing with the cosmos. There is no difference between your breathing and the breathing of the rain forest, between your bloodstream and the world's rivers, between your bones and the chalk cliffs of Dover.
– Deepak Chopra

Einstein's spirituality—his "god concept"—was more sophisticated than the common view of a personalized God. He said, "my comprehension of God comes from the deeply felt conviction of a superior intelligence that reveals itself in the knowable world." His religion was an attitude of cosmic awe and a devout connection with the harmony in nature.

There is a universality to Einstein's cosmic experience that is closely akin to that of Buddhist monks. He believed that these experiences are so intense that they transform the individual in a fundamental way.

The earth on which we live is more than four billion years old—which is enormous compared to man's sojourn on it. Subtle conditions of light, temperature, water, and a proper mix of the elements more than a billion years ago led to the birth of life on this planet. During this evolution, nature proved herself to be all powerful.

We too have been nurtured by nature, and at times we can control Mother Nature. We have the choice to destroy her or protect her and make her even more beautiful. A joint perspective of spirituality and science can point to a set of values guiding us to make positive choices for ourselves and for our planet.

As we explore the values of some of the great spiritual teachers, let us make note of our connectivity with the rest of the Universe and sensitize ourselves to our common origins. When we connect to the living things upon this earth—the trees, grass, and flowers of every hue—we expand our understanding of our connection to this vast Universe. As a result, we also connect to empathy and find the strength to follow our values.

Try It Now Writing Exercise #31
What is the spiritual or religious truth you were raised with?

_____

_____

_____

_____

_____

_____

_____

What is your current belief system?

_____

_____

_____

_____

_____

_____

Do your values reflect your belief system?

_____

_____

_____

_____

_____

_____

My Daily Practice
· Try It Now Writing Exercise #31.
· Review the Daily Conscious Living Plan. Review your vision statements in the categories you chose. Look over the things you are focusing on in each category.

Journal:
· Journal 15 to 30 minutes.
· Set one intention for the day that reflects something you chose from the Daily Conscious Living Plan.
· Get a visual. Close your eyes and visualize yourself doing this one thing on your plan. Really feel it!
· Happy List: Write about one or more things that went well today. What made you happy? Add it to your "Happy List."

Day 26

Clarifying Values: Gandhi

In prayer it is better to have a heart without words than words without a heart.
– Mahatma Gandhi

It is interesting that Gandhi was born in India about ten years before Einstein was born in Germany. Einstein often spoke of Gandhi's peaceful movements in South Africa and India to gain freedom from prejudice and oppression. He spoke of Gandhi as "A leader of his people, unsupported by any outward authority; a politician whose success rests not upon craft or mastery of technical devices; but simply on the convincing power of his personality; a victorious fighter who has always scorned the use of force; a man of wisdom and humility; armed with resolve and inflexible consistency, who has devoted all his strength to the uplifting of his people and the betterment of their lot; a man who has confronted brutality and the dignity of a simple human being and thus at all times risen superior. Generations to come, it may be, will scarce believe that such a one as this ever in flesh and blood walked upon this earth."

Gandhi lived from three deep commitments: universal love; ahimsa (non-violence); and satya (truth). Gandhi also held the belief that no individual, no group or nation, whether poor or rich, should be without gainful employment. He believed that everyone should have the creative opportunity to do something that gives meaning to their lives. He, like

Mother Teresa, identified with the poorest of the poor. He, like Jesus, believed that love was stronger than hate. Gandhi said, "to see the universal truth face to face one must be able to love the meanest creation as oneself…for me the road to salvation lies through incessant toll in the service of my country and humanity."

Try It Now Writing Exercise #32
How do your values align with those of Gandhi?

_____

_____

_____

_____

_____

_____

_____

What would living in truth and non-violence look like for you?

_____

_____

_____

_____

_____

_____

_____

How do you engage in conflict?

_____

_____

_____

_____

_____

_____

_____

What is the primary value you want to bring into the world?

_____

_____

_____

_____

_____

_____

_____

My Daily Practice
· Try It Now Writing Exercise #32.
· Review your Daily Conscious Living Plan and vision statements. Is there something you need to let go of in order to pursue your plan?

Journal:
· Journal 15 to 30 minutes.
· Set one intention for the day that reflects an activity that you chose from the Daily Conscious Living Plan.
· Close your eyes and visualize yourself doing the activities you have chosen from your plan. Feel the feelings you would have engaging in these actions.
· Happy List: Write about one or more things that went well today or made you happy. Your "Happy List" should be getting longer!

Day 27

The Seeds We Plant: Mother Teresa

Let us always meet each other with smile, for the smile is the beginning of love.
– Mother Teresa

Much has been written about Mother Teresa. One of the qualities she embodied, like Gandhi, Jesus, and other spiritual leaders, was a deep commitment to the poor and to non-violence.

According to the book *Mother Teresa—The Inspiring Story And Lessons of Mother Teresa*, by Anthony Taylor, Mother Teresa was raised in a family that supported the deep faith she exhibited throughout her life. In her early days in the convent, she taught high school for girls from the poorest families in Calcutta. In 1946, Mother Teresa experienced a calling that would forever transform her life. She said that she was riding a train to a retreat when Christ spoke to her and told her to abandon teaching to work in the slums of Calcutta, aiding the city's poorest and sickest.

After six months of basic medical training, she voyaged for the first time into Calcutta's slums, with no more specific goal than to help "the unwanted, the unloved, the uncared for." Over the course of the 1950s and 1960s, she established a leper colony, an orphanage, a nursing home, a family clinic, and a string of mobile clinics. In 1979, Mother Teresa was awarded the Nobel Peace Prize in recognition of her work "in bringing help to suffering humanity." What she accomplished was done through faith. Like other spiritual leaders, she touched millions of lives through her unwavering commitment to love and humanitarian efforts.

Sometimes we feel that the values and level of faith of these "spiritual masters" is simply unattainable for the rest of us. But if we look carefully at our own life path, we might find ways to embody these values in our everyday lives.

A friend of mine was deeply affected by Mother Teresa's mission. Early in his career he took time off to volunteer with his daughter at Mother Teresa's Home for the Dying and Destitute, a hospice in Calcutta. This experience was his first exposure to people who were dying. Being completely present to another human in this loving way was completely new to him. He was amazed by how the Sisters of Charity and other volunteers devoted love and caring to complete strangers. He realized that when people are dying in a matter of days, and you do not speak the language, all that can be done is to be present and offer a measure of comfort, loving presence, and dignity to their passing.

Reflecting on his experience in Calcutta, he realized that he had learned to become fully present to another person by the administration of the gift of loving kindness. He saw the dignity loving kindness adds to the human experience, for both the giver and the receiver. He could never have predicted that the spark that was lit from his work in Calcutta would come full circle. He now does hospice work at a facility in the city in which he lives, bringing meaning into his own life as well as to those making that spiritual transition.

In the end, all we have left to give is love. We never know when an experience is going to leave its mark, or how it will eventually play out at another juncture in our path. The seed planted in my friend flourished at another time and place, serving a higher purpose in the grand design for himself and for others.

Try It Now Writing Exercise #33
How do your values align with those of Mother Teresa?

_____

_____

_____

_____

_____

_____

_____

_____

What is something that you would like to implement in your own life on a micro level that reflects these values?

_____

_____

_____

_____

_____

_____

_____

My Daily Practice
- Try It Now Writing Exercise #33.
- Review the Daily Conscious Living Plan. Review your vision statements and the things you are focusing on in each category. Can you find a stretch for yourself?

Journal:
- Journal 15 to 30 minutes.
- Set one intention for the day that reflects something you chose from the Daily Conscious Living Plan.
- Close your eyes and visualize yourself doing this one thing on your plan. Really feel it!
- Happy List: Write about one or more things that went well today. What made you happy? Add it to your "Happy List."

Day 28

Defining My Spiritual Heritage: Jesus Christ

A new command I give you: Love one another. As I have loved you,
so you must love one another.
— Jesus Christ

In examining the lives of these deeply spiritual figures, I am struck by the similarities between them. Those of us who grew up in Western culture have a lot of familiarity with Jesus. Even within the belief systems of those who embrace Judeo-Christianity, there are varying opinions as to the facts versus the symbolism in Jesus's life.

Jesus was born into the Jewish heritage and faith. In his human life he demonstrated his moral teachings through the practices of loving God, loving his neighbor, and doing to others what you would have them do to you. He was a brilliant teacher, prophet, and movement founder. He was considered a radical social and political figure as well as a healer.

Like Gandhi and Mother Teresa, Jesus served the poor. His friends were beggars, prostitutes, and the very ill. He was a single individual making a big impact.

According to religious scholar and author Marcus Borg, in *Meeting Jesus Again for the First Time,* Jesus's resurrection is God's "yes" to Jesus and "no" to power. Borg explains that powerful people killed Jesus and that his death is vindicated by his resurrection and liberation from earthly powers. Christ, as a Lord, is the path of personal and existential liberation from the lords of his world. In addition, Borg discusses the resurrection as symbolic of the transformation to new life—an internal dying and being reborn. This resurrection is symbolic of the internal spiritual process that is at the heart of the Christian path.

Jesus taught the path of dying to an old way of being and being born into a new way of being. Borg points out that there is a "remarkable congruence between the way he taught and the way his life ended."

Try It Now Writing Exercise #34
How do you align with the values of Jesus?

_____

_____

_____

_____

_____

_____

_____

Do you implement any of these values in your life? If so, which ones?

_____

_____

_____

_____

_____

_____

_____

What value do you want to focus on more?

_____

_____

_____

_____

_____

_____

_____

As we move forward in our path of transforming negative thoughts and feelings, we become mindful of how all of the dots start to connect. If our small shifts in perception and changing negative thoughts transform our vibration in the field of energy that surrounds us, we also affect everyone else, either directly or indirectly. This awareness of our interconnectedness is added inspiration in our ability to create something completely new. We are seeing through a new lens, but we are also grounded in a new way of being in the world.

This understanding creates an exciting array of new choices. It raises the bar and highlights the importance of how we consciously live our lives, driven by intention and our thoughts and beliefs, positive and negative. We have come full circle, understanding how the creation of new experiences begins with digging deep to discover our own truth. We can no longer be held captive by the untruth of our negative thoughts.

My Daily Practice

· Try It Now Writing Exercise #34.
· Review the Daily Conscious Living Plan. Review your vision statements and the things you are focusing on in each category of the plan.

Journal:

· Journal 15 to 30 minutes.
· Set one intention for the day that reflects something you chose from the Daily Conscious Living Plan
· Close your eyes and visualize yourself doing this one thing on your plan. Really feel it! Find a picture that represents this thing. Keep it by your bedside.
· Happy List: Write about one or more things that went well today. What made you happy? Add it to your "Happy List."

Day 29

Becoming Conscious: Carl Jung

Every advance in culture is, psychologically, an extension of consciousness, a coming to consciousness that can take place only through discrimination.
– Carl Jung

Carl Jung was born in a rural region of Switzerland in 1875. He was a very lonely child, mostly interacting with the natural world surrounding him. He realized at a very early age that the world is full of unseen forces.

Jung is best known for his work with the conscious, the unconscious, archetypes, the shadow self, dreams, and synchronicity. He believed that the conscious was a minor contributor to our behavior.

The unconscious consists of the personal unconscious and the collective unconscious.
The personal unconscious is the terrain of personal memories, feelings, and behaviors. It is also where we store what we learn in our lifetime. For example, in learning to read, we first learn letters, then how to string those letters into words. Eventually, without conscious intervention, the strings of letters become words and the strings of words become sentences. The words flow without conscious intervention. This pattern is also true of behaviors learned as an adult, such as driving.

The collective unconsciousness is ancient wisdom—all of the images and behaviors that have been repeated throughout the history of mankind, as well as into the future. This is where archetypes reside. The collective unconscious contains information that can be accessed by anyone at any time. It appears to have no limits in time or space. That is, it can access information that was recorded by primitive people as well as information about events that have not yet taken place.

Archetypes refer to images and behaviors related to people in our current or past lives. These images and behaviors can be rooted in cultural heritage or personal knowledge. For example, the father archetype might refer to a patriarchy or to your particular father.

We all have different archetypes that influence our lives. These archetypes usually correspond to a certain stage of our psychological development, and are useful in enacting transition and transformation.

Try It Now Writing Exercise #35
What are some things that you unconsciously do by "rote"?

_____

_____

_____

_____

_____

_____

_____

What are some things you could do with more conscious awareness?

_____

_____

_____

_____

_____

_____

_____

Try It Now Writing Exercise #36
List some archetypes that have been a part of your life.

_____

_____

_____

_____

_____

_____

_____

What archetype would be useful to you at this point in your journey? Research this archetype.

_____

_____

_____

_____

_____

_____

_____

My Daily Practice
· Try It Now Writing Exercise #35, #36.
· Review the Daily Conscious Living Plan. Review your vision statements and the things you are focusing on in each category. Can you find a stretch for yourself?

Journal:
· Journal 15 to 30 minutes.
· Set an intention for the day that reflects one thing you chose from the Daily Conscious Living Plan.
· Close your eyes and visualize yourself doing this one thing on your Plan. Really feel it!
· Happy List: Write about one or more things that went well today. What made you happy? Add it to your "Happy List."

Day 30

My Dream Life: Carl Jung

Where love rules, there is no will to power; and where power predominates, there love is lacking. The one is the shadow of the other.
– Carl Jung

Jung's theory says that dreams exist at the boundary between the conscious and the unconscious. All consciousness emerges out of the unconscious—and dreams are one of the magical boundaries between the two. As we record and interact with our dreams, a bridge begins to form between these two regions. The more access we have between the conscious and the unconscious, the more growth and change accelerates.

Jung said, "We dream a world into being that dreams us into being." Major changes in our lives appear in symbolic form in our dreams long before they are evidenced in outer life. Often dreams are so rich in meaning that it is impossible to fully understand them at first. Later, other dreams will pick up small threads of the changes that are coming.

Jung felt that the primary function of dreams was to serve as an unconscious compensation to our conscious attitude. In other words, dreams help us balance polarities. If your conscious attitude to a situation is largely one-sided, then a dream may take the opposite side. If your conscious attitude is more balanced, the dream may reflect that balance.

In his book *Consciousness Regained*, experimental psychologist Nicholas Humphrey points out that dreams center on emotional accuracy, not physical accuracy. That is why dreams seem so real. Since we experience dreams as real we should be able to learn from them in much the same way that we learn from our conscious experiences.

Honor your dreams. Review them and try to figure out what they mean. In analyzing your dreams, trust your emotions. They are your best guide as to whether you are on the right track. Don't let your rational mind force you to a conclusion that your feelings tell you is incorrect.

Try It Now Writing Exercise #37
Before you go to sleep tonight, write about a situation you are struggling with. Ask for guidance from the Divine or the collective unconscious about the situation.

_____

_____

_____

_____

_____

_____

If you remember your dreams when you wake up, write them down now.

_____

_____

_____

_____

_____

_____

_____

Did you receive any guidance through your dreams? (It's okay if you didn't. These things take time!)

_____

_____

_____

_____

_____

_____

_____

My Daily Practice

· **Try It Now Writing Exercise #37.**
· **Review the Daily Conscious Living Plan. Review your vision statements and the things you are focusing on in each category. Can you find a stretch for yourself?**

Journal:

· **Journal 15 to 30 minutes.**
· **Set one intention for the day that reflects one thing you chose from the Daily Conscious Living Plan.**
· **Close your eyes and visualize yourself doing this one thing on your Plan. Really feel it!**
· **Happy List: Write about one or more things that went well today. What made you happy? Add it to your "Happy List."**

Day 31

Understanding My Own Darkness: Carl Jung

Even a happy life cannot be without a measure of darkness, and the word happy would lose its meaning if it were not balanced by sadness. It is far better to take things as they come along with patience and equanimity.
– Carl Jung

The shadow is an important part of Jung's work and an important part of looking at the self. In Jung's view, we spend the first half of our lives developing a healthy ego so that we are able to function satisfactorily in the outer world. With the ego developed, we can then allow ourselves to turn away from the world and find our deeper selves. Individuation requires us to pass through both of these stages. Until we have dealt successfully with the world, we can't find the deeper spiritual side of our personality.

The shadow self consists of traits that we hold in the unconscious. These traits are buried so deep inside us that we do not want to look at them. In acknowledging the shadow self, we acknowledge our fears. As we've discussed, acknowledging a fear is an important tool in not letting that fear control our behavior.

Shadow figures are usually people we intensely dislike or disrespect. We are often afraid of these figures because of how they represent aspects of ourselves. For example, if I meet someone ultra-controlling, I have to look at that aspect in myself. I know I embody that trait to some extent, but I do not have to take it to the extreme presented to me through the shadow. The gift of the shadow is that it gives me the opportunity to acknowledge the trait in myself so that I can manage my own behavior. Once we acknowledge the shadow or fear, it loses its power and becomes something we can control rather than something that controls us.

The difficult part of managing the shadow is that even when we project the shadow on to another person, we have a tendency to deny that we are doing it. Furthermore, how do you distinguish between true injustice and shadow anger? Shadow anger will have an unreasonable quality to it, which is different than the more righteous anger that you experience from true injustice. The angrier a person makes you, the more sure you can be that you are encountering your shadow.

Try It Now Writing Exercise #38
Write about one of your fears.

_____

_____

_____

_____

_____

_____

_____

How does this fear play out in your life?

_____

_____

_____

_____

_____

_____

_____

My Daily Practice
· Try It Now Writing Exercise #38.
· Review the Daily Conscious Living Plan. Review your
  vision statements and the things you are focusing on
  in each category. Can you find a stretch for yourself?

Journal:
· Journal 15 to 30 minutes.
· Set an intention for the day that reflects one thing you
  chose from the Daily Conscious Living Plan.
· Close your eyes and visualize yourself doing this one
  thing on your Plan. Really feel it!
· Happy List: Write about one or more things that went
  well today. What made you happy? Add it to your
  "Happy List."

Day 32
Shaping the Story

*When people say they are looking for the meaning of life they are
really looking for a deep experience of it.*
– Joseph Campbell

Joseph Campbell's work, which spans over fifty years and
twenty books, discusses the invisible realm from which
imagination and inspiration guide us in shaping our lives.

As a mythologist with a metaphysical slant on life, a doctor
of things beyond appearances, Campbell dedicated his life
to mapping out the journey of the soul. He highlighted the
perilous territory to be traversed, not by the faint of heart,
but by the stout of heart. He believed that the symbolism in
myths can act as a guide to help us find our way. "The way
out is the way in," he stated.

Campbell described the hero's journey as "a hero ventures
forth from the world of common day into a region of
supernatural wonder: fabulous forces are there encountered
and a decisive victory is won: the hero comes back from
the mysterious adventure with the power to bestow boons
on his fellow man."

We all take this difficult journey at some point in our lives,
perhaps many times. It is important to make a conscious
choice to be present for the journey. Negative thoughts
and emotions can keep us stuck in the journey, as forward
movement is blocked by negative emotion. It's inevitable
that, at some point, we'll feel negative about our situation.

The challenge is in how we respond. Journaling or therapy can help us make sense of our journey, downloading negative emotions to clear the way for new thought.

Both Jung and Campbell recognized the power of myth in our lives. They certainly aren't the only ones. In a historic conference in San Francisco, entitled "From Ritual to Rapture," Jerry Garcia confessed on stage to Joseph Campbell his feelings about the similarities between ancient mystery festivals and rock concerts: "They didn't know what they were saying, and we don't know what we're saying either, but we think we're saying the same thing."

Try It Now Writing Exercise #39
Can you identify a myth that is a part of your life?

_____
_____
_____
_____
_____
_____
_____

Does your culture identify with a certain myth?

_____
_____
_____
_____
_____
_____
_____

My Daily Practice
- Try It Now Writing Exercise #39.
- Review the Daily Conscious Living Plan. Review your vision statements and the things you are focusing on in each category. Is there something you need to let go of in order to succeed?

Journal:
- Journal 15 to 30 minutes.
- Set one intention for the day that reflects something you chose from the Daily Conscious Living Plan.
- Close your eyes and visualize yourself doing this one thing on your Plan. Really feel it!
- Happy List: Write about one or more things that went well today. What made you happy? Add it to your "Happy List."

Day 33

Discovering Resilience: The Hero's Journey

We must be willing to get rid of the life we've planned, so as to have the life that is waiting for us.
– Joseph Campbell

The Hero's Journey is the ultimate call to adventure. It is a journey that we all take at least once in our life, and many of us take several times. Engaging in the journey is a choice. We often refuse the call because we are busy or don't feel worthy, and sometimes we simply ignore difficult circumstances and hope the situation will go away. The Hero's Journey is significant because it tells us that the only way out is through. Going "through" a situation is the opposite of running away. It helps us get in touch with our real emotions, giving us an opportunity to heal wounds and address fears. It also gives us the chance to develop the great gift of resilience, which teaches us that we have the ability to deal with any situation.

The Stages of the Hero's Journey:
1. The Ordinary World: The hero is in their everyday environment. Life pulls the hero in different directions, causing stress.
2. The Call to Adventure: Something shakes up the hero's situation and the hero must face the beginnings of change.
3. Refusal of the Call: The hero tries to turn away from the adventure.
4. Meeting with the Mentor: The hero comes across a

mentor who offers training, equipment or advice that will help on the journey.

5. Crossing the Threshold: The hero commits to leaving the Ordinary World and enters a new region or condition with unfamiliar rules and values.
6. Tests, Allies, and Enemies: The hero is tested and has to evaluate allegiances.
7. Approach: The hero and newfound allies prepare for the major challenge.
8. The Ordeal: The hero confronts death or faces their greatest fear.
9. The Reward: The hero takes possession of the treasure won by facing death.
10. The Road Back: The hero is driven to complete the adventure.
11. The Resurrection: The hero is tested again before being able to return home. Polarities that were once in conflict are resolved.
12. Return with the Treasure: Transformation! The hero returns home bearing a treasure that has the power to transform the world just as the hero has been transformed.

  •

Everyone's Hero's Journey looks different. My journey was ignited by the death of my young husband, Tom. I was thrust into the unknown and went through the phases of the Hero's Journey, ending with Transformation. There have been other Hero's Journeys in my life, but none as distinct as this one.

It's easy to get trapped by negative thoughts and feelings when faced with a Hero's Journey. It is important to acknowledge your negative feelings, become aware of the wounds they touch, and make a conscious effort to heal that part of yourself. Refusing the Hero's Journey keeps you in the ordinary world without the gift of transformation. The Hero's Journey is an opportunity to develop your trust in a Higher Power, cultivate resilience, and find new ways of being in the world.

Try It Now Writing Exercise #40
Think about a Hero's Journey you have taken. What did it look like?

_____

_____

_____

_____

_____

_____

_____

Can you identify the incident that pushed you into this journey?

_____

_____

_____

_____

_____

_____

_____

What were the biggest challenges you faced?

_____

_____

_____

_____

_____

_____

_____

What did the outcome look like?

_____

_____

_____

_____

_____

_____

_____

My Daily Practice
- Try It Now Writing Exercise #40.
- Review the Daily Conscious Living Plan. Review your vision statements for the categories you chose. Look over the things you are focusing on in each category.

Journal:
- Journal 15 to 30 minutes.
- Set one intention for the day that reflects something you chose from the Daily Conscious Living Plan.
- Get a visual. Close your eyes and visualize yourself doing this one thing on your Plan. Really feel it! Write about how your life would be if you lived out this intention.
- Happy List: Write about one or more things that went well today or made you happy. Add it to your "Happy List." Wow!! This list is getting long—are there some repeats?

Day 34

It's All About Choices: The Fork in The Road

You enter the forest at the darkest point, where there is no path. Where there is a way or path it is someone else's path. You are not on your own path. If you follow someone else's way you are not going to realize your own potential.
– Joseph Campbell

The fork in the road represents the big decision points in our lives. In my own journey, one of the forks represented a career decision. I was trying to choose between several career paths, and ultimately made the choice that resonated with my heart and my desire. I became a social worker. It has proven to be the right path for me. The more I pay attention to the path, the more I learn. There are times when I don't understand why I am moved to make a particular choice, but the reason is always made clear in hindsight. No experience is wasted.

The Hero's Journey offers us many opportunities to make choices. My experience is that when I choose the "right path," things seem to flow pretty easily. There may still be challenges, but I always find support to face those challenges. On the other hand, when I choose a path or fork that is not congruent with my journey, the doors do not seem to open. I feel stuck—like I am trying to move through mud!

The fork in the road can be a frightening place. What lies ahead is unknown. In choosing a new path, you affirm your willingness to undergo major life change and personal transformation.

Try It Now Writing Exercise #41
Think of a path you did not take in your life. If you had chosen this path, where do you think you would be?

_____

_____

_____

_____

_____

_____

Would you be a different person than you are now?

_____

_____

_____

_____

_____

In hindsight, would the other path have been better for you?

_____

_____

_____

_____

_____

_____

Why or why not?

_____

_____

_____

_____

_____

_____

_____

My Daily Practice
· Try It Now Writing Exercise #41.
· Review the Daily Conscious Living Plan. Review your vision statements in the categories you chose. Look over the things you are focusing on in each category. Does anything need to change?

Journal:
· Journal 15 to 30 minutes.
· Set one intention for the day that reflects something you chose from the Daily Conscious Living Plan.
· Think about the changes you are making in your life. Close your eyes and visualize yourself doing one thing on your Plan. Really feel it!
· Happy List: Write about one or more things that went well today or made you happy. Add it to your "Happy List." Wow!! Notice the repeats on your list—these are things that consistently make you happy.

Day 35

Finding Your Flow: How "Inner Space" Fuels "Outer Space"

The best moments usually occur when a person's body or mind is stretched to its limits in a voluntary effort to accomplish something difficult and worthwhile. Optimal experience is something that we make happen.
– Mihaly Csikszentmihalyi

You have done a lot of work!! You've taken in a great deal of information and added valuable tools to your toolkit. The new behaviors you have put into place should be getting easier. Each time you engage in your new behaviors, you build new neural pathways. You are developing a different flow.

You have learned a lot about science, spirituality, energy, and your blocks—those heavy, old and tired negative thoughts and beliefs that keep you stuck. You are no longer sleepwalking. You are aware of your patterns and desires. You are actively engaging in transformation. You are *Waking Up*!

You have become aware that the "inner game" fuels the "outer game." When your inner and outer lives are in alignment, your values and beliefs reflect a deep trust in the universe. The external self, the ego, can take you just so far. You have to silence the ego in order to be present and become the quiet witness of the powerful internal connections that spark the world around you.

What takes you into **flow**? Flow is that coveted place where magic happens. It is the artist fully immersed in painting a portrait or the athlete engaged mind and body in running a race. It feels spiritual. It taps into the limitless possibilities of your mind and body, where endorphins flow and renegade thoughts develop. The "a-has" just pop into your mind. It's automatic. Thoughts seem to emerge one after the other. You are no longer in control. You let go. You breathe. You feel. You get lost in the moment.

So how do you flow? You're already doing it! Over the last thirty-five days, you have worked on reprograming your pathways so flow begins to "FLOW" out of your subconscious.

My epiphanies, my flow, come when I am writing or walking in nature. I see a waterfall, a tree, or a cloud and this triggers a feeling that connects the lanes, like a new super highway. Writing helps to pave the path as you find your flow. Journaling connects your thoughts and pushes you to dig deeper and to reflect on your inner life.

Finding your flow takes practice. Remind yourself to take that quiet moment. Stretch and let go. Sit down, breathe, and find your **FLOW!**

Try It Now Writing Exercise #42
Over the past thirty-five days, you've added new behaviors to your life. Think about a time when these behaviors have come naturally. When are you in FLOW?

_____

_____

_____

_____

_____

_____

_____

What does flow feel like to you?

_____

_____

_____

_____

_____

_____

My Daily Practice
· Try It Now Writing Exercise #42.
· Review the Daily Conscious Living Plan. Review your vision statements in the categories you chose. Look over the things you are focusing on in each category. Does anything need to change?

Journal:
· Journal 15 to 30 minutes.
· Set one intention for the day that reflects something you chose from the Daily Conscious Living Plan.
· Think about the flow your changes are bringing to your life. Close your eyes and visualize yourself doing one thing on your Plan. Really feel it!
· Happy List: Write about one or more things that went well today. What made you happy? Add it to your "Happy List." As your list continues to grow, notice any patterns.

Day 36

Creating a Legacy

The life you live is the legacy you leave.
– Lynne Twist

Every day, you write the story of your life and make choices that carve the imprint you will leave into the world. What is the legacy you are leaving for others to feel, to follow? How can you pay conscious attention to your legacy?

Becoming conscious and waking up changes your imprint and legacy. If you want to be a passionate and loving participant in life, you must set the intention to live that way.

In Lynne Twist's book *The Soul of Money*, she writes that we create our most lasting legacy not in what we leave behind, but in the way we live, especially the way we live with money. An impoverished spirit leads people to believe that money defines who they are and who they can choose to be in life. Twist's work led her to the conclusion that, regardless of financial resources, in order to thrive and cultivate a meaningful life, we must draw from other and deeper resources.

Most of us experience conflicts about money and the calling of our soul. We may be in harmony about many things in our life, but things get messy when we enter the domain of finances. How do negative feelings about money impact your life? Can you change those thoughts? Our culture revolves around money and it is an important factor to consider in thinking about your legacy.

Try It Now Writing Exercise #43
How do you allow resources to flow through your life?

_____

_____

_____

_____

_____

_____

_____

What are the money myths that you believe or live out of?

_____

_____

_____

_____

_____

_____

_____

Is there a myth you need to change?

_____

_____

_____

_____

_____

_____

My Daily Practice
· Try It Now Writing Exercise #43.
· Review the Daily Conscious Living Plan. Review your vision statements in the categories you chose. Look over the things you are focusing on in each category. Does anything need to change?

Journal:
· Journal 15 to 30 minutes.
· Set one intention for the day that reflects something you chose from the Daily Conscious Living Plan.
· Think about the flow the changes are bringing to your life. Close your eyes and visualize yourself doing one thing on your Plan. Really feel it!
· Happy List: Write about one or more things that went well today. What made you happy? Add it to your "Happy List." Notice the repetitions and patterns.

Day 37

Living The Legacy

You can't connect the dots looking forward; you can only connect them looking backwards. So you have to trust that the dots will somehow connect in your future. You have to trust in something— your gut, destiny, life, karma, whatever. This approach has never let me down, and it has made all the difference in my life.
– Steve Jobs

As we make choices to define our legacy, it is important to think about where we put our time, money, talent, and attention each day. If we are living an unconscious life, we just keep going by rote. The days blur and we don't remember or notice the details.

When my young husband, Tom, passed away many years ago, we had not even had time to think about or consider a legacy. Death was thrust upon us before we had an opportunity to plan for the long term. We had certainly never discussed how I might navigate the rough terrain after his death with three young children to raise.

However, because of the way he lived his life, he had created a legacy. Tom had a deep respect for and good relationship with money. As an investment executive, he wanted to make money for his clients, who became his friends. He lived a harmonious life, loving the outdoors, respecting nature, and really living life. He was a devoted husband and father, laughed a lot and loved good humor.

When he was dying, an endless train of people came to visit him in hospital. I had no idea how many lives he had touched. It was not just his business colleagues, but people who worked in his building, college friends, tradesmen, it was endless. He made everyone feel respected and special. He developed a legacy of love, kindness, respect, and humor. His attention to everyone in his life was evident. That was his legacy.

At the time, I was not fully aware of how his legacy impacted me or our children. In retrospect, I can see how his values contributed to my choices in both how I continued to raise our children and how I treat others. I had a front row seat witnessing how a legacy is built: through communication, respect, and love. Lynne Twist's words ring true—we create most of our legacy through the way in which we live.

Try It Now Writing Exercise #44
What is the legacy you want to leave?

_____

_____

_____

_____

_____

_____

_____

My Daily Practice

· **Try It Now Writing Exercise #44.**
· **Review the Daily Conscious Living Plan. Review your vision statements in the categories you chose. Look over the things you are focusing on in each category. What needs to change?**

Journal:

· **Journal 15 to 30 minutes.**
· **Set an intention for the day that reflects something you chose from the Daily Conscious Living Plan.**
· **Think about the new flow in your life. Close your eyes and visualize yourself doing one thing on your Plan. Really feel it!**
· **Happy List: Write about one or more things that went well today. What made you happy? Add it to your "Happy List." Wow!! This list is impressive.**

Day 38

Alignment: Sculpting Your Purpose

I want to put a ding in the universe.
– Steve Jobs

One of the gifts of waking up is gaining clarity about the things that are important to you. Clarifying your personal vision will ultimately help you define your purpose. Your purpose may change over the course of your life, but there will be a consistent theme that seems to bubble beneath the surface.

We all search for meaning and significance. The incremental changes we make in becoming conscious move us toward a life filled with meaning. We begin to live from our inner truth, knowing that our actions make our life count. You make a difference in the world. You have been given unique talents and skills. You can use those talents and skills to make the world a better place.

Your life purpose is like a personal mission statement. It's like a compass; it keeps you on track and influences your decision-making process. Having a purpose helps you experience happiness. Without purpose, your life is left to chance.

As you think about your purpose, consider the following questions from an article written by Kathleen Barton:
1. Describe yourself: What words describe you and your values? Some examples might be: honest, integrity,

enthusiastic, loving, faith, harmony, intelligent.

2. Define your gifts: What are your passions? What excites or energizes you? What are you really good at? When are you happiest?

3. Reflect on your life: What are your talents and hobbies? What work activities do you enjoy most? Think about all the things you have done—it's probably a long list! What common denominator do you see running through your life?

4. Describe your legacy: What kind of legacy do you want to leave? How do you want to be remembered? Think about this on both a micro and macro level.

5. Put it all together: What do all these statements say about you? Do you see a congruent theme? Take some quiet time to think about this. Read back over your vision statements—are they in harmony with your values?

Your purpose statement should be one or two sentences. Include your passions, things you enjoy, what you are good at, and what you want to bring to the world.

Here are a few examples of purpose statements:

· Bill Wilson exists to encourage and inspire others to a life that is founded on science.

· Margaret Jones is here to protect the rights of underprivileged people and bring the light of hope to their lives.

· Tom McClure lives to provide food for people and protection for his family.

Try It Now Writing Exercise #45
Write your one or two sentence purpose statement. This may evolve over time, but from where you are right now, what do you think your purpose is?

_____

_____

_____

_____

_____

_____

_____

My Daily Practice
·   Try It Now Writing Exercise #45.
·   Review the Daily Conscious Living Plan and your vision statements. How are you doing? Does anything need revision?

Journal:
·   Journal 15 to 30 minutes.
·   Set one intention for the day that reflects something from your Plan.
·   Close your eyes, feel with your whole body how it would feel to do this thing. Smile as you see yourself doing it. Place your hand on your heart and say Thank You to the Divine for letting this wonderful change come into your life.
·   Happy List: Write about one thing that made you happy today. Put it on your "Happy List." Feel the gratefulness throughout your body.

Day 39

The Thread: Gratitude and Grace

When you arise in the morning, give thanks for the morning light,
for your life and strength. Give thanks for your food and the joy
of living. If you see no reason for giving thanks, the fault lies with
yourself.
– Tecumseth, Shawnee Native American Leader

Over the last thirty-nine days, you have taken brave steps
navigating a sustainable path to change. Gratitude is a
necessary and powerful component in sustaining change. It
is one of the highest forms of love and counteracts feelings
of separation and distance. Gratitude operates through a
Universal Law that governs life. It keeps us connected to
God, the source of all good things.

All the major religions practice gratitude. History is full of
people who practiced gratitude — Gandhi, Mother Teresa,
Jung, Jesus, Lincoln, Martin Luther King, Jr., to name just a
few we've considered together.

Old patterns of negative thinking can block us from feeling
and expressing gratitude. That is why I ask you reflect
on something you are grateful for as part of your Daily
Practice. Thinking about what you are grateful for attracts
more of that quality to your life. Your gratitude is like a
magnet. YOU become magnetic.

Establishing gratitude as a habit allows compassion and
grace to flow from you. Negative thoughts cannot grow

when the mind is filled with gratitude, compassion, and grace. Feeling compassion for yourself and others opens the doorway for love.

Try It Now Writing Exercise #46
What are the changes you have made that you are the most grateful for?

_____
_____
_____
_____
_____
_____
_____

How have these changes impacted your life?

_____
_____
_____
_____
_____
_____

Have you thanked your soul and spirit for guiding you to make these changes? Take some time now to thank yourself.

_____
_____
_____
_____
_____

My Daily Practice
- Try It Now Writing Exercise #46.
- Review the Daily Conscious Living Plan and your vision statements. What is next for you?

Journal:
- Journal 15 to 30 minutes.
- Set one intention for the day that reflects something from your Plan.
- Close your eyes, feel with your whole body how it would feel to do this thing. Smile as you see yourself doing it. Place your hand on your heart and say Thank You to the Divine for letting this wonderful change come into your life.
- Happy List: Write about one thing that went well today. What made you happy? Put it on your "Happy List." Feel the gratefulness throughout your body.

Day 40

My Toolkit: Putting It All Into Practice

Gurus can teach us skills and techniques. They can increase your understandings of life, death and the spiritual planes, they can help remove fears and obstacles. They can point out the doorway, but it is we who must go through the door.
– Brian Weiss

Remember when you started this journey forty days ago? You are not the same person today that you were then. Not only have your chemicals and cells changed, but you have made yourself vulnerable, acknowledged what you want to change, examined negative thoughts and beliefs, and found the courage to make changes. Look in the mirror and acknowledge this new person. Remember Michael Jackson's song, "Man in the Mirror"?—"If you want to make the world a better place, take a look at yourself and then make a change." That is YOU!

You know that every action impacts not only your life, but the whole Universe. You are committed to living in the present with awareness and consciousness. You are the master weaver of your life, writing your story day after day. Making small shifts gives you the courage to make greater shifts. The more you practice your new habits, the more deeply you will feel them becoming a part of your "natural" program, like driving a car. It will become easier and easier.

Now that you have started this process of transformation, your awareness of your own negative blocks will surprise you. You will not want to tolerate the energy they bring into your life. I encourage you to work through the journal again as you discover new potential for growth and change.

Some 2,500 years ago, Lao Tzu spoke of the "four cardinal virtues." By practicing these virtues, we come to know the truth of the Universe and realign ourselves with God or Source. The first virtue is reverence for all of life. This includes love and respect for yourself and others. The second virtue is natural sincerity. This means being honest with yourself about your life, and not making excuses about why things are not working out.

The third virtue is being gentle with yourself and others. Practicing kindness is the best way to shift from negative to positive. The fourth virtue is supportiveness. This means being of service whenever possible, shifting the focus from serving yourself to serving others. Incorporating these four virtues into your life gives you the ability to reconnect to God or Source daily and to make different conscious choices.

As you move forward, take some time each day to think about the four virtues and the foundation you've built over these past forty days. Keep weaving new threads until you have woven a new cloth. The cloth is a continuous work of art—and remember—you are the weaver!

Try It Now Exercise #47
Look in the mirror. What do you see? Smile at yourself.
Congratulate and thank yourself for having the courage
to make some changes. What else does this brave person
want to change?

_____

_____

_____

_____

_____

_____

_____

My Daily Practice
- Try It Now Writing Exercise #47.
- Review the Daily Conscious Living Plan and your vision statements. What is next for you?

Journal:
- Journal 15 to 30 minutes.
- Set one intention for the day that reflects something from your Plan.
- Close your eyes, feel with your whole body how it would feel to do this thing. Smile as you see yourself doing it. Place your hand on your heart and say Thank You to the Divine for letting this wonderful change come into your life.
- Happy List: Write about one thing that went well today. What made you happy? Put it on your "Happy List". Read through you list and take in all those moments of happiness you've experienced through this period of transformation. Feel the gratefulness throughout your body.

Made in the USA
Columbia, SC
18 December 2019